THE PEARL OF PIPARO
MY LIFE: AN EVENTFUL JOURNEY

PEARLITA

Avocado Publishing

The Pearl of Piparo
My Life: An Eventful Journey
All Rights Reserved.
Copyright © 2022 Pearlita
v3.0

The opinions expressed in this manuscript are solely the opinions of the author and do not represent the opinions or thoughts of the publisher. The author has represented and warranted full ownership and/or legal right to publish all the materials in this book.

This book may not be reproduced, transmitted, or stored in whole or in part by any means, including graphic, electronic, or mechanical without the express written consent of the publisher except in the case of brief quotations embodied in critical articles and reviews.

Avocado Publishing

ISBN: 978-0-578-27079-1

Cover Photo © 2022 Pearlita. All rights reserved - used with permission.

PRINTED IN THE UNITED STATES OF AMERICA

DEDICATION

*This book is dedicated
to the memory of
my father,*

Emmanuel "Mannie" Douglas

TABLE OF CONTENTS

Foreword i
Conclusion ii
Review v
Preface vii
Acknowledgements ix

Part 1
Chapter 1: The Journey Begins 1
Chapter 2: My Grandma 5
Chapter 3: Mannie, My dad 11
Chapter 4: Tantie Edith 22
Chapter 5: Ma 30
Chapter 6: Schools 37
Chapter 7: Places Lived 48
Chapter 8: Finding A Way 53
Chapter 9: My Siblings 56

Part 2
Chapter 10: Confronting the Challenges 71
Chapter 11: The Howards 78
Chapter 12: Forging Ahead 82
Chapter 13: IDC/MDC 85
Chapter 14: My Husband 92
Chapter 15: Preparing to resign 97
Chapter 16: Business Experience 103

Chapter 17: Overcoming trials 112
Chapter 18: Settling down 119
Chapter 19: Testimonies 123
Chapter 20: Final Thoughts 146

FOREWORD

Where do I begin the story of a Pearl in formation? Let me begin at the end. Pearl and I had not spoken for over three decades. Then she calls me. "I want you to write the foreword for my book." "Why me?" I ask. She answers without hesitation, "The Spirit moved me to call you." With those words, that thirty-year gap between us evaporated. I could not refuse my friend, Pearl Spring, and as I read her life story, I understood why I was chosen. It is a joy to write this foreword.

Her story is one of a country girl, rising from poverty and brutish conflictual forces, to become a successful entrepreneur, wife, mother and citizen. The reader gets deep insights into life in Trinidad in the middle of the 20th century, as Pearl captures with brutal honesty, her move from pillar to post as she crafted a better life.

She embraces a simple and direct style of writing, free of complex academic constructs, intrigues, or other linguistic and literary distractions. This orientation comes straight from the school of life itself. The reader feels, more than reads, Pearl's major life transitions – growing up, schooling, marriage, work, following her passion. We experience school pranks, bathing in the natural world of cocoa fields and coffee plantations, early experiences of running water, morris chairs, electricity, trams, cane-juice, conch shells, street fights and scriptures (used most forcefully when arguing with neighbours). It all takes place across our country from Chaguanas to Farnum Village, Tabaquite, Ecclesville, Hardbargain, Marabella, Laventille, Tunapuna, and finally, her story settles in Valsayn.

If this sounds glamorous, it is not her intention. The truth is far from this. The challenges of no home, no meals, no books and no space to call her own, never dulled her instinctive drive to improve her lot. Pearl was a problem-solver and she learnt from these experiences. Her almost incessant wrestling with daily problems furnished the impetus for her growth. And grow she did, driven always by her mantra - Live simply and with purpose.

I have always believed that living in a plural society carries additional civic responsibilities. To live authentically, one must risk, learn, reach out – not merely tolerating the other but seeking to understand a different way of being. There is strength in diversity, if only we can use it to grow us, not divide us. Pearl's story turns these words into life itself. Her spiritual experiences, friends, food preferences and clients reflect her embrace of our country's rich diversity. I couldn't help but smile at her assertion that the best menu for her, in the school feeding program, remains curried channa, pumpkin chokha, paratha roti and curry mango.

CONCLUSION

"Hope is like a road in the country: there was never a road but when many people walk on it,
the road comes into existence." (Lin Yuting)

Pearl's message is one of hope eternal. At 18, in the midst of all kinds of adversities – ill health, a broken family, debt and death – Pearl prevailed, firm in her belief that nothing stays broken forever in the presence of God.

I recommend this book for its unvarnished realities, simplicity, and the hope that it evokes. It urges us to be patient, but also to do something. Be part of a play larger than self. Connect with purpose and community. Indeed, she uses her story to issue some tacit invitations to us all.

- Life has its ups and downs. Adversity is not permanent. We can always use our strength and energies regardless of circumstance.

- To grow, to learn, to improve – they all become easier when we hold God as our master.
- Hope is both a belief and a practice.

Let's accept these invitations, for within them lies the alchemy of Pearl's formation and our troubled world needs many more pearls.

Nazeer Sultan
Former Banker
Management Consultant &
Professional Toastmaster

REVIEW
by **Cecil Spring**
Educator, & Director
Avocado Restaurant Ltd.

This is the enthralling story of a young lady who, when she turned eighteen, decided to walk away from a life of poverty and family separation. Her entire life is one of victory over hardships. She progressed from being a Nanny and Housekeeper to Executive Secretary and Office Manager at a prestigious governmental agency, and eventually to being the owner and CEO of a well-known catering establishment.

My wife's story will inspire readers, and even our own children, to recognise that adversity is not an impenetrable wall but only a challenge to overcome. Adversity, though it may last a while, is still temporary; but joy and success, with the help of God, is permanent.

Pearl's life's story reminds us of a poem by Longfellow, **A Psalm of Life**, which reads in part:

Lives of great men all remind us
We can make our lives sublime,
And, departing, leave behind us
Footprints on the sands of time;

Footprints, that perhaps another,
Sailing o'er life's solemn main,
A forlorn and shipwrecked brother,
Seeing, shall take heart again.

REVIEW
by **Winston Drayton**
Business Consultant

This book demonstrates how a woman of the soil chose her own path, without knowing what the outcome would be. It speaks to the power of faith, love of God and his creation, and endurance.

From a young age, Pearl knew what she wanted - she had a dream. This dream led her to take the route commonly available to women in those days - secretarial skills, which brought her to the Management Development Centre as a Typist, a Stenographer, an Executive Secretary, and eventually an Office Manager. It was here that she was inspired by the great Clyde James and Grace Talma (both Management Consultants) to follow her dream, in which cooking, and entrepreneurship were to play a great part.

Pearl's "sweet hand" became the foundation on which she built a successful and fulfilling business in the food industry. *Avocado Restaurant Ltd.* became synonymous with good creole food in East Trinidad. This later morphed into an innovative catering service known for its mouth-watering cuisine. Later, this business would become a dependable provider in the School Feeding program.

Whether it's her loving husband, her children, her siblings, or her extended family in church, everyone can attest to having benefitted from her deep and enduring love, given liberally. Trust me when I say: Pearl is truly a beacon of God's grace and a shining example of fortitude in sickness, health or wealth. Her book will tell you the rest. Enjoy!

PREFACE

My Father's Legacy

This book is dedicated to the memory of my father, Emmanuel "Mannie" Douglas, known to his three daughters as *Dad*.

Dad fought vigorously to take control of his children even though the courts had given custody to our mother. Although he was a skilled carpenter, he worked all his life in a sand quarry to provide for his children. My Dad had an alcohol problem but never allowed this to hinder him from carrying out his fatherly role.

As young children we disliked him, and often wished for the day we would return to live with our mother. As adults, we came to appreciate what a great father he was, as he had tried with everything available to him to give us the best life possible.

My job as the family cook was to prepare breakfast and lunch at 4.00 a.m. each day for my Dad before he left for work. Perhaps he saw that I was that way inclined why he made me the gift of his precious tawah (otherwise known as a platin), which is a flat round baking sheet made of iron. This is what he had used to bake his cassava bread and other flat breads that he liked.

Dad had very little material wealth to leave for his children, so he thought that his gift to me of this tawah may someday be put to good use. While Dad was not able to leave anything substantial for us, he instilled in us some of life's precious values; for example, our Sunday night prayer meetings, based on the Anglican tradition, which we continue up to this day.

Perhaps my dad foresaw my destiny because I graduated from being the village cook - cooking for various social events - to small-scale catering, then to restaurant proprietor and caterer.

Mannie's two granddaughters, my two girls, attended St Joseph Convent, the school he liked. My first girl went on to study at the University of Texas at Austin, and the other to Penn State University. My first daughter majored in Petroleum Engineering and is at present employed in that field. My second daughter majored in Economics and Finance.

She, however, decided to follow her mother's footsteps and so pursued a Diploma and an Associate degree in Culinary Arts and Science at Le Cordon Bleu Culinary Institute, in Paris. She is now well-positioned to take on the role of C.E.O. of Avocado Restaurant Ltd, a position I am sure would have made Mannie proud indeed.

My regret today is that my Dad didn't live to see his dream of seeing his three daughters take their place in the world, nor his granddaughters, for that matter. I owe a huge debt of gratitude to my father, and I will always be grateful for the role he played in our lives.

ACKNOWLEDGEMENTS

I give glory and honour to God for his direction and guidance along the way, and as Paul said in 1Corinthians 15:10: "But by the grace of God I am what I am, and his grace which was bestowed upon me was not in vain; but I labored more abundantly than they all; yet not I, but the grace of God which was in me."

I also wish to express my heartfelt gratitude to my dear husband, Cecil, for all his moral support and encouragement.

To my children, Abiola and Fayola, thank you for your patience and understanding.

"For I know the thoughts that I think toward you,
saith the Lord, thoughts of peace, and not of evil,
to give you an expected end."

Jeremiah 29:11

CHAPTER 1
THE JOURNEY BEGINS

That morning the train had just passed, and Sylvia had just returned empty-handed because the train had not slowed down long enough for her to pull off some of the sugar cane. We all looked forward to that sugar cane each morning. This was part of our early morning routine. Part of our breakfast was lost; but we still had our roast bakes and salted butter, with our shining bush tea which we also had every day.

Around mid-morning, I looked up the dirt track and there was my father, a tall, dark, handsome man, walking towards the house. We were all so happy to see him, knowing that whatever gifts he was bringing, we would all share in them. After exchanging greetings with my aunt, he took us to the nearest parlor (a small shop) and bought that famous cake that we all loved—dark-coloured, with a hard crust and sprinkled with white sugar--also known as "belly full". My father made sure that everyone partook of this delight.

The conversation then began: "Well," he told my aunt, "I am taking my children with me."

To this my aunt replied, "Oh no, you can't. My mother dropped them with me with strict instructions that they stay here until she returns."

"I understand," my dad said, "but they are *my* children. I have a new home for them, and I have come in peace to collect them."

My Aunt knew my father and immediately realized that it was pointless trying to put up a fight, so she reluctantly agreed and grabbed all our things. Right then I remembered my pink purse that my mother had purchased for me.

"Come on, Chile, we will pick that up another time," my father said, as he hustled us out of the house with my little sister, Earla, in his arms.

I was three years old, and my sister was one year, when we boarded that train from Chaguanas to Tabaquite that morning. I remember sitting near to an old Spanish lady who had a terrible cold and from time to time would spit into a cup. As a child I had no idea where the train was heading nor how long it would take before we got off. I was just hoping it would be soon. My Dad seemed happy to hold his two kids in his arms once more as the train rocked from side to side. He told us we were going to a place called Farnum where we would meet our new stepmother. Her name was Miss Edith, but we were to call her Tantie. He said she was wonderful, she would cook us nice meals, she would take us to school, and we would all be a happy family.

After a long train ride going through what seemed like a never-ending, dark tunnel, we finally arrived in Tabaquite and boarded a taxi for Farnum. We arrived at a large barrack-type building with different families occupying what looked like different apartments. The entrance to our apartment was a small area with a dirt surface and a large hammock. This led to a small living room with a wooden table, four chairs and another piece of furniture which I later found out was a dinner wagon. There was one bedroom leading into a small kitchen with a fireside. There was a ladder leading to an upper floor which, I later learned, led to a cocoa house.

Enter Ms. Edith, not looking anything like my mother nor my aunt. She was wearing a long-flowered dress, and a head tie with a small bow at the back. She had on small, hard rubber sandals that she called a sapat.

She wore a small smile as she looked down at us and said, "So these are the children?"

"Yes," my dad replied. "This one is Pearl, and this here is Earla."

"Okay Polly and Ola (that was her pronunciation), come and get something to eat."

I don't remember crying or laughing. All I was thinking was what Grandma would say on her return when she realized that we were gone. Ms. Edith, or now Tantie, soon realized that she was now faced with a ready-made family. We, on the other hand, were getting used to our new surroundings.

Here on earth, you will have many trials and sorrows,
but cheer up, for I have overcome the world."
John 16:33

CHAPTER 2
MY GRANDMA

My grandmother had lived in Todd's Road all her life. We were told that her mother had come from Barbados. Her maiden name was Lewis, but she had married a Johnson. I never knew Grandpa Johnson because he died long before we were born. Grandma was the village midwife, who delivered many "grand babies", as she proudly called them. She was also called upon to attend to all the pregnant women in the village.

Gramma, as she was called, was cruel to all her grandchildren. Just call her name and her grandchildren would tremble. Her favorite form of punishment was using a guava whip on us, following which she would have you kneel on a grater. She worked in a tobacco field in Todd's Road, and she would be often seen smoking her tobacco pipe. One pipe was grey, and the other was white. I would often admire her filling the pipe with tobacco, lighting it and then begin puffing. One day, I thought to myself, I would be able to do this.

I remember the day my sister, who was about five years old, broke one of her pipes. We all sat around and watched in horror as she was severely beaten. Gramma often punished her grandchildren without good reason. I remember coming from school one day and seeing a lot of coconuts under a tree. In my childish reasoning, I felt that Gramma could use these in the kitchen, and so I collected them and took them home to Gramma. I was accused of stealing and was severely beaten.

One day, I remember admiring Gramma working hard at her sewing machine and thinking how skillful she was. The dress material had red polka dots, and she was just attaching the sleeves when she suddenly stopped and pulled me aside giving me several slaps, accusing me of thinking that she was spending the allowance given to her by my mother to buy some dress material for us. It took me several years, and countless other beatings, to understand what that meant.

Gramma's granddaughter, Claire, very often would arrive on a Monday morning by the train from Enterprise to Todd's Road to attend the Todd's Road R.C. School. She would spend the week with Gramma to have easy access to school. We would look out for the train bringing Claire on Monday mornings because that meant Gramma would spend more time disciplining Claire and less time focusing on us.

Gramma disliked all her in-laws, and often got into physical fights with all of them. Her daughters, whenever there was a misunderstanding with their husbands, would often call on Gramma. I recall fearless Gramma would always end up in a fight with my father. If my father felt he couldn't tangle with an old woman, he would often resort to some form of wickedness, like hiding her purse or some other piece of her possessions.

Gramma had four girls and one boy of her own. She was openly overprotective of her boy. She went berserk when her son met and married an Indian girl who had already had a previous relationship and two children. However, her dislike for this girl never stopped them from having a long-lasting marriage. I remember stories of Gramma putting her hand on this girl even when she was pregnant.

One of Gramma's daughters got pregnant at an early age. This girl was beaten so badly that she ran away from Gramma and away from the village. Her family never saw her again. Gramma never saw her again and never bothered to look for her. It is believed that she got together with her baby's father. She never returned to her family because of her fear of her mother.

Another one of her daughters died while giving birth. The baby, however, was taken by her father, whose family raised the child until she was about twelve years old. She never knew her Gramma until one day when Grandma arrived on her guardian's doorstep demanding that she hand over her grandchild. That day Gramma met her match. The lady demanded that she be compensated for the many years she had raised the child. It took a lot of reasoning by neighbors who intervened and stopped what could have resulted in a fight.

I remember the time a young man came to live in the apartment next door to Gramma on Fletchers Road. In order to get to his apartment, he had to pass close to Gramma's house. This he did daily without acknowledging her or any of the neighbors. My grandmother thought this was rude and she set out to teach him a lesson. At this stage, Gramma was a member of the Spiritual Baptist faith, so she knew all the songs they sang. She took the opportunity to teach us all the songs and had us singing and clapping all night so loudly that Mr. No Name was forced to come over, introduce himself, and ask that the noise stop. This is when I learnt to sing all of the Spiritual Baptist songs and their heavy chants.

One of Gramma's first grandchildren was Theresa. She had the misfortune of living with Gramma all her life. For some reason she never did things to please Gramma and always felt the butt of her grandmother's whip. Many times, we were helpless witnesses to her many floggings. I remember distinctly the night Ma Johnson was in one of her moods and after one of her beatings she called on Theresa to stop her tears.

In those days, most houses had a dirt yard, and all the neighborhood children would be bitten by a small flea, otherwise known as 'jiggers', that lodged mainly between the toes, and this caused a lot of uneasiness, itching and scratching. On this particular day, the itching became too much for Theresa. Ma Johnson, of course, had the remedy for this. She got a razor blade and decided to cut away the jiggers and rub salt and pepper between the toes. Theresa screamed in agony.

I could hear my grandmother shouting, "Chile, if you don't shut up, I will put you outside." Theresa crawled downstairs where I am sure there were more jiggers. Her bawling got louder and louder until Gramma became so angry that she took a whip and beat Theresa out of the yard. Theresa went under the nearby shop, limping and screaming. A Good Samaritan heard her cries and called the authorities who took her to St Mary's Orphanage. From all reports, her mother and sisters kept in touch with her.

All Ma Johnson's children would drop off their children with her, whenever they were having problems with their husbands.. So, they all had stories to tell of Gramma's cruelty. The worst experience was when, after we had a shower, Gramma would begin to comb our hair -- an experience none of us would ever forget. She pulled and scratched so hard, that at the end, our head would be on fire.

I remember at one stage my mother and her husband broke up and she decided to take all the furniture and hide them at Gramma's place. Gramma had no problem accommodating her. But weeks after she made up with her husband and went back to Gramma to retrieve her furniture, she was prevented from even stepping into Gramma's house. She was forced to return to her husband without her furniture.

Gramma was married a second time, to Mr. Festus. I remember him with his long, flowing grey beard, and a cruel anti-child face. Mr. Festus was a Seventh Day Adventist. So, for the entire day on Saturdays, he and Gramma would pray and read the Bible. I remember being hungry for the entire day because not only was there no cooking, but there was no sign of food. The area where they lived was Arena, a small village between Chaguanas and Todd's Road. I remember the yard being hard and of a reddish color. The only things that grew there were cashews and guavas. My cousin, who would sometimes visit Gramma, would often pick guavas, and share them with me and my sister.

I believe Gramma was first a Spiritual Baptist, then she converted to being a Seventh Day Adventist and went back to being Spiritual Baptist. When the time came for Gramma to go on the mourning ground, we would have to pack our clothes and bundle them on our heads and walk to my uncle's house to sleep. These were fun nights because my uncle (her eldest son) had several children our age. Sometimes we would go outside the Baptist church in the village and try to mimic their moaning and chanting.

We had fun days whenever we spent time with my uncle's children. From them I learnt to "leepay" houses, which is a form of plastering, using cow dung. We made the mixture using cow dung and dirt for plastering the outside and the floor of the hut. Upon completion, it had a nice finish but a horrible smell. It was by my uncle I learnt how to make a "Chulha", which is a fireside made using the same mixture.

"The parents you had were the ones He chose,
and no matter how you may feel, they were
custom-designed
with God's plan in mind and bear the master's seal."
Russell Keller.

CHAPTER 3
MANNIE, MY DAD

Enterprise was where my parents, Ma and Dad, lived. Together, they had three girls. My mother was a housewife, while my dad was the bread winner. Ma was born in Todd's Road and sometimes worked in the cocoa and coffee estate in Talparo. Her marriage to my father was her second marriage. She was first married to Mr. Edwin Philip and they had three sons. My mom was very attractive, brown in complexion and, like her mother, was always well dressed.

My father was 20 years older than my mother. He was born in Tobago, and he would often tell us that he was born on the high seas, probably on the Bocas, on the way from Tobago to Trinidad. A lot of his family had come from Tobago and had settled in Central, in Enterprise. He was a carpenter, and so too were both his brothers.

As a child, I remember people saying my father was a very wicked man. At one time he owned a very long ladder and very often he would gladly lend it to others in the area. One of his friends refused to grant him a similar favor and one day he came and borrowed Dad's ladder to climb a tall building. My father gladly loaned it to him, but when a heavy shower came, he removed the ladder and left his friend on top of the building, screaming for help.

I believe our household was a very violent one. Fighting was the order of the day. On one occasion during a fight, my father pelted my mother with a flower pot; she returned the favor with a vase. My sister, who was a baby, got struck above the eye. The blood and screams failed to stop the encounter. The following day, my father, knowing she was going to take the train to get my grandmother, took a side of each of her shoes to work with him to make it difficult for her to travel.

As I grew older, I often wondered why my dad hated anyone to talk loudly in the garden. I later found out that he himself did little gardening but would enter other people's gardens at early hours of the morning and steal their produce. There is the story of dad's uncle, Uncle Gurry, who would punish my father severely when he was a child. My father vowed that when he grew up, he would return the favor. When Dad got his first job, he invited his uncle to his house for drinks. Uncle Gurry, not knowing that there was still bitterness in my dad's heart, drank until he was completely drunk. My father took out a stick which he had hidden and started beating him, all the while reminding him of the many times he mistreated him as a child.

Another instance was when Dad invited to our home a group of friends towards whom he had some bitterness. As they sat around the table and made all their speeches, they decided to make a toast. As they drank, they soon realized that the drink was cooking oil. My father had to run for his life. Dad enjoyed playing such childish pranks on his friends.

Dad was a 'stick-fighting man'. This skill he inherited from his father who was a renowned stick fighter in Trinidad. His nickname, according to my dad, was 'Ten Ten Britain'. Needless to say, carnival time was always a sad time for us. This is the time when the country would have a lot of stick fighting competitions. Dad had his special stick which he had well-oiled and placed in a corner. There were special songs that they sang during a stick fight. Whenever we heard any of those songs, we would always be sad because we knew that aroused something in our father which he couldn't resist. In the end, he would come home with severe cuts and bruises on his face.

Because Enterprise was an area where they grew a lot of cashew nuts, we always had a special hole dug in the ground for roasting the nuts. On one occasion, when we were roasting cashew nuts, one of my cousins placed my sister's feet into the fiery furnace. Needless to say, she was badly burnt, and my cousin had to go back to his house before my father returned home. As a child I witnessed so much violence that I developed a strategy to defend myself. I remember bending down to the concrete floor and sharpening my teeth to attack anyone who would try to attack me or my sisters.

Mannie, as my dad was commonly called, was also a musician. I have never known him to play in a music band, but I have heard him play the trumpet and the cuatro. He loved to sing and even though I never knew him to go to church, he knew every hymn in the Anglican hymn book. Dad spoke Spanish fluently and he often gathered with some of his local Spanish friends to sing all the old parang songs. Dad also spoke Hindi, and some of his old Indian friends conversed with him only in Hindi.

Dad loved the ladies, especially those of a lighter hue like my mother. However, I would often hear him complaining that he had a problem with their cooking and their housekeeping. I remember the day he came home, and at that time he was living with this red, Spanish-looking, young woman, and realized that at 11.00 a.m., we hadn't eaten breakfast. He was so enraged that he immediately asked her to leave.

As children, we would often peek into Dad's bank book. One day we were pleased when we saw that his bank balance was $7,000. We found out later that he never had that amount in his account. In fact, he always kept an old book with a balance of $7 to which he added on a few zeros to show his false worth to potential girlfriends. Dad had many girlfriends but never brought them home for fear they wouldn't be good for his children.

My dad's first, and only property he owned, was a small wooden house on approximately one lot of land in Enterprise. In fact, all his brothers who had migrated from Tobago, had bought properties in Enterprise. I remember him having a few clumps of sugar cane which he would juice himself in his own man-made juicer. To us, as children, freshly-juiced cane juice tasted just great. In those days, juicing sugar cane for home consumption was very popular.

In addition, most of those old-time houses consisted of a wooden, matchbox-type frame, with a long plank leading to the kitchen area. I remember fighting my sister one day over a condensed milk tin. The tin was taken from inside the sugar bowl and had lots of sugar on it. The plank broke, landing both of us on the ground. Rain had probably fallen the night before, so the ground was wet and muddy. We were soon both a muddy mess.

I never knew my dad to engage in gambling, but he drank heavily. I don't know whether this led him to sell his property twice to two separate buyers. I also don't know whether this was done intentionally, but this resulted in his having to evade the law; so, he left Enterprise, and started a new life in the countryside.

Dad disliked my grandmother fiercely, and whenever he couldn't find a way to get back at her, he would attempt to destroy something, or somebody, she loved. On one such occasion, he targeted her two grandsons. Evans and Eric had lived with Gramma for a while, and she loved these two because their mother had died in childbirth; in fact, they practically grew up with her. As teenagers, they both landed jobs at the cement company in Chaguanas.

One bright sunny afternoon while we were sitting outside and waiting on Gramma's pot bake to finish roasting, two policemen came to our house and arrested both Evans and Eric for stealing. This attracted the attention of everyone because these boys had been accused of stealing two bags of cement from the company where they worked. After days of my grandma crying and paying countless visits to the police station, she was able to get the boys released. It was discovered that no cement was missing from the company, but my father had purchased the cement, planted them at my grandmother's house and reported them stolen. This was done to cause my grandmother grief and heartache. The boys vowed that before they died, they would one day take revenge on my father.

My dad, Mannie, was fearless. He had no problem confronting men, whether they were big or small. He was, however, terrified when it came to snakes. I remember one day when we were already in our early teens, we heard a loud eerie noise coming from a nearby plum tree. When we looked outside, we realized it was a large multi-colored snake holding a bird in its mouth. We called out to my father to rescue the bird. Dad instantly gathered up his manly strength, picked up a hoe and ran towards the tree. When he got to the tree he was overtaken with fright. Before he could fire the first blow, he collapsed there and then, giving the snake time to escape. That day we all laughed so much that he himself had to join in the laughter.

There was a gentleman living in one of the huts adjoining our hut in Farnum. Very often as children we would look in at him over a small verandah, and we would tell my stepmother how he would remove his pants and would show us his private parts. This, we found out later, she had relayed to my father. And my father had a way of getting even with people when he was drunk. So, this particular day, dad was having drinks with this gentleman, whose name was Smokie, and we weren't very happy because Dad's voice began to change. We always knew when Dad had too much to drink because his voice would change.

For some reason, Dad asked Smokie to run back home and bring him his stick; I guess to show off some of his skills. According to Smokie, Dad wanted the stick in the corner by the bedside, the one with a cloth tied to its head. I wasn't keen on my father giving any stick fighting display, so I told him he couldn't have it. Smokie wasn't happy about any child speaking to him in that tone, so he slapped me. The 'slap' was nothing but a slight touch to the face, but knowing my dad would react, I screamed loudly.

This sent my dad running, leaving the rest of his friends behind, and coming to check us. When he realized what had happened, he got the stick himself and began to beat Smokie with it. This resulted in Smokie being beaten to the ground. Friends and neighbors called the police. When Dad realized what he had done, and that the cops were on the way, I don't know how he managed to pretend that he was the one badly hurt; and indeed, he was frothing from the mouth! The result is that the police detained Smokie.

My father loved his children and always wanted the best for us. I don't know whether it was his Tobago upbringing, but for him, education was a top priority. I remember him looking at some girls dressed in convent uniforms and telling us that one day we, too, would be wearing those uniforms. My father hated to hear 'bad' language, and insisted we only use the Queen's English. His idea of education centered around English and Maths only. So those textbooks we had to get for subjects such as Geography, History, or Literature, never mattered to him.

My dad had other names for all of us; for example, when he was mad at me his name was Pearlita; when he was in a good mood, his name for me was Polo. His name for my little sister was Urlit, and his name for my big sister was Roob Roob. We were all smart and athletic in school, but he always had a problem with us getting involved in extra-curricular activities. One day the school was having a big concert, to which parents were invited. My younger sister had a leading role in one of the plays. On the day of the concert, after she had practiced for several weeks, my father decided that she couldn't attend. When the concert was about to start and the principal saw no sign of the main character, he decided to visit her at home. It was only after much begging and pleading that my father allowed her to go. In fact, he decided to go along. Instead of Dad behaving like the other parents and looking on with pride at his daughter's performance, he was outside sitting under a tree with a cutlass in hand, in case anyone interfered with his children.

In secondary school I played netball. My position was defence. I told my father, and he was totally against it. Of course, he wouldn't purchase the uniform. The uniform was a lovely, short white dress, cut along the A line, with blue stripes on the hips and flowing boxed pleats. When the netball captain realized I wasn't getting the uniform, they decided to purchase it using school funds. Many times, after matches, when my friends would remain either celebrating victories or just chatting I would have to leave them and hurry home. One day I got home late, and when my father found out I was playing netball, he came upon us quietly while I was relating the evening's event, grabbed the uniform and shredded it to bits. I had problems trying to explain to my teacher what had taken place. Luckily, we had almost come to the end of the season with few matches left to be played.

Living with our father, especially when we entered teenage years, was rather difficult. All the things other girls did, we would be forbidden to do. All the fashionable clothes, and accessories we liked and other people wore, we couldn't have. I guess my father felt that we were growing up too quickly and he would not be able to handle it.

There was a particular trick I used on my parents very successfully for years. If, for instance, I wanted to visit a friend and was sure I wouldn't get permission, I would tell Ma I was going by Dad and vice versa. There was this day in question when all my friends were planning to go downtown for the carnival celebrations and our plan was to stay at home, away from all the celebrations. Like a true Trini, even though I was not allowed to go, I vowed that day I would find a way. Luckily, I found a lovely gold men's ring in a taxi. I took it to the pawn shop and got $2.00 for it. That was my answer to prayer.

Carnival was Monday and Tuesday, so I told my father I was spending the carnival weekend by my mother. Actually, I was going by my friend, Jennifer, who lived in Princess Town. As children, we always covered for each other, so I told my sister Ruby where I was going. I went home that Friday after school with Jennifer. We did all the girl things that I was not accustomed to, because she lived with her mother who gave her a little more freedom. We shopped, shampooed our hair, and practiced new hairdos, among other things.

In the middle of our excitement, her mother called out to me, "Pearl, your father is outside."

I replied in disbelief, "That's a laugh."

To my surprise, I looked up and saw my dad, wearing his lily-white shirt and his black flannel pants, standing in the doorway. My friend's mother tried to assure my dad that I was quite safe staying with her and pleaded with him for me to stay, but he was not moved. I later learnt that my sister Ruby, who had become a little jealous, told my father about my plans. My father hired a taxi, traversed the whole of Princess Town, enquiring of any Williams until he found Jennifer's house. That was the end of my carnival!

There was a time when we were all given a project to write our autobiography. I completed mine and my friend, whom I considered a much better writer, wanted me to read hers. I took home sheets of paper with her life story on it. According to her, she put her heart and soul into this piece of writing. When I got home my dad saw me reading it and thought that it was suspect. It had to be something pornographic that had my interest. In those days, comic books and True Confessions magazines were forbidden in homes. My dad waited until I had read it and placed it on a shelf. He went quietly, lighted a match, and attempted to burn it. Being the agile teenager that I was, I quickly ran to him as he lit the edge and kicked it out of his hand. I had problems explaining to Sylvia the next day how I got the edge burnt.

My father became a violent drunk when he drank excessively. When he was sober, he was the most caring, loving father. However, when he was drunk, he was transformed into a lunatic. Weekends was never a good time for us, especially during the period when my stepmother had left. On Friday evenings when 6:00 p.m. arrived and dad had not come home, we knew we were in for a rough night.

One must remember the houses were approximately quarter of a mile apart, so we were cut off from the neighbors around. Most times, drivers would stop and tell us that our father would be somewhere along the route, either stumbling home or lying drunk at the side of the road. He had a special chant that he used to keep him going. This we learnt from the young boys in the area: "Bee deep bor; bee deep bor." They even mocked us with this name.

Dad's drunkenness on Friday and Saturday nights was a sight to behold—pure theatre! Most times when Dad would eventually arrive home, he would have his dinner, which he ate ravenously like Magwitch, the convict in *Great Expectations*. He would eat unashamedly putting his mouth directly into the plate. He would eat four times what he would normally eat, and a few minutes later complain that we did not feed him. At that point you had two choices: either prepare some more food or run for your life. My elder sister always chose the former. I would always prefer to run, because the cooking process meant having to light the fireside with the help of a pooknie, which was a piece of iron pipe used to blow air to fan the flames, especially when the firewood was sometimes very wet. The places you had to run to were through the woods, areas you wouldn't venture during the day; but that way you would be safer from Dad's rage.

Sometimes, he would sleep face down in the same plate, would get up every ten minutes, stamp his feet and quarrel with his deceased mother, saying to her, "Woman, woman, leave me alone!" and "Backside! Backside!" Our prayers as children were that God would take my father. Many times, people in the area would enquire about our mother, because they couldn't understand how we lived under such conditions.

One night, around midnight, it rained heavily. We were worried because we hadn't seen our father. That night, many drivers stopped and told us that our dad was drunk and lying in a drain somewhere on the road. I was about twelve, my older sister around 14, and my younger sister around 8, so it didn't make sense going to his assistance. That night, we cried because the character we saw finally stumbling up the road was not our father. He looked like a man possessed.

Our old house had about five steps leading into the house, with a drain filled with water running under the steps. Dad got to the house but couldn't climb the steps. The three of us held on to him and tried to pull him up the steps. On the first attempt, he had almost reached the top when he collapsed, fell down into the water, getting a huge gash above his eyes. We had to lift him out of the water and try again. When he was almost at the top and into the house, he fell on the other side again, hitting his forehead again and causing blood to gush out. At this point, the three of us were wet, muddied and bloodied. The next day, Dad vowed he would never drink again. He was sober for about two weeks. Then he started to drink again, and although this time it was only wine, this was not the end of his drinking habits.

It was a Sunday afternoon when Dad brought home Moonika, whose real name was Monica. She was a tall, skinny, brown-skinned Indian girl whose father was my dad's "rum buddy". Apparently his wife had died, leaving him with this nine year old girl. Dad thought it a good idea to help his friend by taking the little girl to live with his family. I don't know whether the decision was made when they were both under the influence, but Moonika came to live with us and our stepmother. Her father never visited, after she moved in.

Moonika arrived during the summer holidays, so we were overjoyed to have another sister to play with. We played hop scotch, moral, rounders, pitched marbles; and best of all, we played in the rain. At the end of the summer holidays Dad realized he had a problem on his hands because Moonika had never attended school and was not interested in doing so. In addition, she used a lot of obscenities which she perhaps had learned from her father.

Moonika lived with us for approximately two years, and we knew that Dad was getting weary of having to explain to people why she was not attending school. It was becoming obvious to all that she didn't like our lifestyle, nor our foods. We knew she was not happy because often she would remember her "Moi" (mother) and her "Poi" (father).

One afternoon as the 3.00 p.m. bus stopped in front our house, on its way to Tabaquite, to our surprise Moonika jumped into the bus with just the clothes on her back and, as far as we knew, no money in her pocket, and disappeared. We never found out whether Dad got any explanation from her father, but we, my sisters and I, never heard of her again.

Interestingly, dad remained fit and healthy all his life. He was never sick! In fact, he never visited a doctor nor a dentist. Perhaps the reason for his fitness and agility was partly because he worked in a quarry for years and walked six miles each day to and from work. When there was a fete in the district, Dad was always the talking point the next day. Apparently, he was light on his feet and knew all the latest dance moves.

"A step parent is a truly amazing person.
They made a choice to love another's child
as their own."

CHAPTER 4
TANTIE EDITH

Tantie Edith, my stepmother, played an important role in my life. Tantie adopted us when I was approximately three years old, and my sister only one. She was born somewhere in the Williamsville area. Most black people in Trinidad came from one of the islands, but Tantie's family was spread all over, from Farnum to Hardbargain, from Mayo to Flanagin Town, from Sisters Road to Brothers Road, from Stone Road to Fifth Company. I feel that she was somehow related to the Merrikins, the group of African-Americans who had fought with the British against the US in the War of 1812 and couldn't return to the United States; instead, they were given lands and livestock in Trinidad.

Tantie was a devoted wife and hated when my father introduced her to his friends as his housekeeper. We used to listen and laugh at her singing because she sang African songs, made her own music and accompanied herself, all the while doing what we thought was an African dance. Tantie was a skilled baker; she would often bake the tastiest breads and cakes using a huge dirt oven or a drum oven to do so. I remember the school principal visited us one Christmas and I was so embarrassed when my stepmother offered him a piece of her Christmas black cake. Imagine my surprise when Mr. Harriet said it was the best cake he had ever tasted. It was only then that I respected my stepmother's baking.

Tantie and her brother worked for the village overseer. Mr. Nobbie, as he was called, owned the estate in the village. He also owned the shop in the area where Tantie would purchase all her groceries. She also worked part time as his maid and cook. This family was an upper class, Indian family and they hired Tantie because she was good at preparing Indian dishes.

My father used to make fun of her because she couldn't read or write. She was only able to differentiate between orange and grapefruit juice because of the colors of the labels on the tins. I remember the day when she reaped bags of pigeon peas and set out for the wholesale market to sell them. My father was furious because when she returned with the grand sum of 12 cents my father realized she had been robbed.

One day, Tantie had us all dressed up to go to San Fernando to witness the carnival celebrations. We were so excited, walking from street to street with Tantie holding on to our hands for we were seeing all the fancy Indians. We had little concern for the bands. All we saw was the people, the colors, the variety of individual costumes. It was all so fascinating to us. That day, we were treated to palettes (an icy treat), ice cream, press (snow cones). She bought whatever we wanted; she was so anxious to please.

A few times we were accosted by fancy devils shouting, "Pay the devil!" Poor Tantie would reach into her purse and pay them. At the end of the day, my stepmother was so broke that she didn't have enough for taxi fare to go back home. She, however, knew that the bus was much cheaper, so we boarded a bus going to Princess Town to overnight by some of her family with the hope of getting taxi fare to take us back home.

In the village where we lived, everybody knew one another. In fact, most of them were related and I would often hear people warning Tantie that the children she opted to raise would one day be ungrateful. Tantie was always nice and understanding. She was never rough, and she never punished us. So much so that I felt comfortable talking to her rather than to my father. My father had a special word to describe certain people. We very often used that word without realizing the real meaning of the word. Tantie would very gently let us know that word was not suited for children to use.

Tantie had a problem dressing us for school. She couldn't comb our hair properly and even though our hair would be freshly done each day, at school we were laughed at and told, "Look at you; all you hair not combed for days." Even teachers realized that all was not well in our family. I remember one teacher took a special interest in us and would often question us about our lives. I would often go and tell my father, who ended up sending Miss Thomas gifts. I remember one of the gifts was a chicken. I had to leave the chicken at a friend's house to give to Miss at the end of the day. I also remember Miss asking to meet my father. I don't remember how this was arranged but I do recall Miss was in the school yard under a tree conducting her reading when my father, all dressed up in his Sunday best, and looking very handsome kept walking up and down the street.

I don't remember how Dad's meeting with Miss Thomas ended, but I do recall that in my innocence, I related the incident to my stepmother and any further rendezvous came to an abrupt end. Dad could no longer send chickens or any other gifts to Miss Thomas.

Tantie used to take us to her cousin's house in Brothers Road. I remember it was a long, picturesque drive on an old Bedford bus. So unaccustomed I was to travelling, that I used to believe the trees and the objects on the road would move. After passing through cocoa fields and coffee plantations and by hog plum trees we would finally arrive in Brothers Road. Her cousin's house was a large wooden plantation type house with fruit trees all around. On that first occasion, they seemed to be happy to meet us and after the initial introductions, they took us outside and showed us around.

We loved our stay with these people. However, there was one aspect I didn't like, and I innocently shared this with my stepmother. One of her cousins, whose name was Baynes, would very often pull me in a corner and kiss me on my lips. All right, I was accustomed with people kissing me, but this one would try to put his tongue in my mouth. I told this to my stepmother who I assumed told my father. That ended our visits to Brothers Road.

One Christmas, everybody was preparing and like everybody else, we were excited. We decided to hang up a pair of Dad's socks, expecting Santa would come and leave us gifts in our so-called stockings. Christmas morning came, and we were so disappointed when we were faced with the same empty socks. Tantie, not knowing what to say and seeing our disappointment, told us the reason why Santa didn't leave anything was because we hung socks instead of stockings. At that age we didn't even know the difference.

That Christmas morning, I got hold of a comb and a piece of silver cigarette paper and began to play music and entertain myself. I remember at that age never owning a toy and therefore never missing one. We would play under the huge cedar trees at the back of the house or sometimes catch fireflies in bottles and listen to their noises.

Tantie was happy with her life, she loved her job—rising early, putting on her sapats, waiting for the conch shell to blow to alert her and her fellow employees it was time to go to work. She was proud of her family name: Outram. She would often boast that anybody with that name in Trinidad was related to her. They all knew us, and we would always visit them with her. I remember one family member who had about six children. Very often, we would visit just when the pot would be almost ready to get off the stove. She would lower the fire, much to our disappointment, until we were gone.

Tantie had lots of chickens. I remember most of them had names. The one I remembered was called Betsy. We never had to buy eggs, and the chickens were killed and prepared only at Christmas. I used to be angry when Dad's supervisor would visit and demand that Tantie boil a few eggs for him.

When my sister was two years old, we were playing with some dry seeds we got from some dried fruit. One seed accidentally went down my sister's ear. As big sister, I tried in vain to remove it. Instead of it coming out, it went further down. Not knowing what to do, I went to my stepmother. Doctors were not accessible in those days, so my sister had to be taken to the hospital. Not knowing her way around the hospital, Tantie had to make numerous visits before she could locate the emergency department where she was able to get help.

It was during one of those visits that we spotted my mother on High Street, selling her sweepstake tickets. Needless to say, I recognized her and ran to her screaming with joy. All I remember was that she was light in complexion, had a shiny gold tooth and she wore glasses. "Ma! Ma!" I shouted, as my mother hugged and kissed us and introduced herself to my stepmother. This was the first time my mother came face to face with the woman who was living with my father and taking care of her infant children.

Ma took us into a nearby parlour where she bought us soft drinks and Marie biscuits, but while we were eating, our mother disappeared.

A few years later, while playing in the backyard, we heard of a lady waiting outside in a taxi wanting to see us. Perhaps it was embarrassing for my mother, because when we got to the car, we couldn't determine whether she was our mother or our aunt. Once again, she had brought us biscuits and sweets, and then disappeared.

At a certain time, I became quite ill. Normally as children when we got sick, Tantie usually would figure out what was wrong and administer her own medicine, but on this occasion nobody could tell what was the nature of my illness. I had no desire to play with friends, had lost a lot of weight, had no desire to eat, and was often sleeping during the day.

When my condition had got really bad, my father before he left for work one day, gave instructions to my stepmother to take me to the doctor. That morning I got all dressed up with my little red shoes, knowing that I was going to the doctor who would give me some injection to make me feel better. I was about seven years old.

The doctor's office was in a district called Mayo, approximately six miles from where we lived in Hardbargain. Those areas were not readily accessible by motor vehicles, so we got up early that morning and began our walk to Mayo, with my step mother holding my hand. Somewhere between Esmeralda and Whiteland as we were about to ascend a little incline, I felt that I could no longer walk. Tantie had to lay me down in the grass at the side of the road. After regaining some strength and getting to my feet, I still wasn't able to walk, so Tantie carried me on her back for the greater part of the trip, occasionally putting me down at the roadside to regain her strength.

At last, we got to the doctor's office. While awaiting our turn, I was lying on her lap and occasionally she would pat me gently to reassure me that all would be well.

Finally, it was our turn to enter the doctor's office. I found myself looking into the smiling face of a short, Asian-looking man with a long grey beard and soft brown hairs on his hands. As I stood up between his legs, I heard him enquire from my stepmother about my eating habits. He told her that I was badly malnourished and gave her a list of the foods a child my age should have, some of which never existed in our house. The list included things such as milk, cheese, eggs, butter, and carrots.

After receiving a painful injection, I was able to leave the doctor's office, this time a little more energized for the walk back home. I don't know how my diet changed, but I never had that experience again.

As adults, my sisters and I regretted how we had treated Tantie Edith, considering she had adopted us as babies. When my oldest sister came to live with us, she pointed out a lot of Tantie's deficiencies: She was old fashioned, and illiterate; nor was she young and attractive as my mother. And most of all she was not *our mother*, and therefore couldn't lay down any rules.

Tantie was so afraid of us that she never quarreled in front of our faces. She would wait for us to leave for school and while she was doing her chores would quarrel to herself, outlining all our faults and swearing what she would like to do to us. Honestly, I was the worst; and so, one day I locked myself in my room and pretended I had left for school.

After she had said all that was on her mind, I opened the door and confronted her. I got the satisfaction of seeing her quiver. I guess this proved her family right—that one day we would be ungrateful!

One day, our Tantie removed herself from our lives, fed up of our disrespect and my father's emotional and physical abuses. She left, taking with her her pension which had helped to upkeep the house. She took all her furniture, leaving us with absolutely nothing. My dad, being the carpenter he was, built us a wooden table and four chairs. He built a wooden settee, which is where we piled our wares, etc. He also built another small table, on which we placed the "chulha", our homemade fireside.

We never knew exactly when our Tantie died. We later found out that she was living with her favorite niece for a while and then moved on to other family members.

When my mother left my father, she left him with the younger girls, that is, my sister Earla, and me; but she kept my older sister, Ruby. Dad vowed that he wanted his daughter and would try everything to get her. One day he went to her school, around 3.00 p.m., just as her school was dismissed. Even though she hadn't seen him for years, she instantly recognized him and went along with him, whereupon he entertained her with a drink and some snacks.

Ruby only realized that she was in danger, after he took her to the taxi stand and placed her books into a car trunk. She immediately ran and left him with her books. That evening dad came home and was at pains trying to explain how he came into possession of Ruby's books.

After a while, when Ma got tired of him trying to abduct Ruby, they agreed to an exchange. He could have Ruby, but she wanted me.

"Sometimes, hurt is a necessary part of God's plan.
In the midst of it, we should remember
that he always has a purpose
waiting for us at the other side of our pain.
If we will be faithful to seek God and obey him
when things are tough, he will be faithful
to help us through it."
Dodie Osteen

CHAPTER 5
MA

My mother, Novelyia, was known by her husband as Lucy, and by her family as Dootsy. To us she was known as Ma. Ma was born in Todd's Road and went to work at an early age in several estates in Talparo. There she met Mr. Philip and had three boys for him. Her first boy, Joseph, she had at age 15. He was followed by Michael and Cecil. She later fell in love, and married my father. They had three children: Ruby, Pearl and Earla.

Their relationship was very toxic. My dad was 20 years older than Ma, and they didn't seem to have anything in common. I knew about the many fights, but never truly understood the reason for them. I remember the day Ma boarded a bus with my sister and disappeared. That evening, Dad came home and found us soaking wet. He then had the problem of seeking help from his family. Then there was the time when he left us with his brother. It had just gotten dark, perhaps around 6.00 p.m., when they decided to put us at the side of the road to wait for our father.

We used to stay by Ms. Edward, a neighbor, who lived opposite to us. Ms. Edward had several grown daughters who treated us very well. I remember we were never satisfied with the meals given to us at her home. I remember flattening the rice in the plate to make it look plenty. So, after Ma had left, the Edwards provided help for a while. It took a long time before Dad eventually got himself a girlfriend. We were so happy that we had another mother that we neglected the Edwards. One day Dad's new lady eventually left, without even kissing us goodbye. As children we didn't know better, so we rushed over to the Edwards not realising that they were upset that we had neglected them during the time our stepmother was there. They chased us out of their yard, reminding us how we behaved when we had a stepmother.

My mother somehow got wind of what was happening to us and one day when Dad had gone to work, she came and collected us and sent us to her mother's. We had our own experiences with Grandma before she decided she wanted to go on the mourning ground. This is when she took us to her sister's house in Chaguanas. It was around this time that our father came and collected us.

Meanwhile, Ma was doing well in San Fernando. She started to sell sweepstakes on the streets and very soon she met her new boyfriend, Mr. Theo. She later moved in with him and managed to open a small parlor. Ma got lucky one day and won a small prize while selling sweeps stake. According to her she was able to purchase a lot of land in Marabella. At that point, she and her boyfriend became serious and build a small wooden house on the land.

We later learnt to call her boyfriend Uncle Theophilus. Uncle Theo, as he was known to us, jointly owned a small restaurant in San Fernando with his brother. My stepfather's brother, whom we called Uncle Toby, was always very kind-hearted. In fact, he permitted me during my school lunch break to have lunch each day at the restaurant free of charge. I would have been about eleven years old, dressed in my little brown San Fernando Girls' E.C. uniform when I used to dine in the main eating area with the rest of customers..

His daughter Joanie was the only other schoolgirl to dine in the restaurant each day. I remember Joanie, in her convent uniform, having her lunch at the cash register. Most times, I would be given a seat at the register when Joanie had already eaten and left. After lunch I was always hoping to meet Uncle Toby because he would always give me six cents, as opposed to the one penny my stepfather would give.

I somehow got the feeling that Uncle Toby was never fond of my mother because he felt that his brother had married "down". His brother, coming from a business family, well-known and well-respected in San Fernando and marrying a sweepstake vendor! I don't think this sat well with him, and what's more, my mother did nothing to prove him wrong.

The restaurant catered for the Pointe a Pierre crowds, and mainly blue collar workers in the area. Their menu listing each day, written on a board outside the building read: Stewed beef/pork, ground provision with dumplings and stewed red beans. This menu stuck with me to such an extent that during a nutrition course at St Gabriel's School's Home Economics class, we were asked to prepare a balanced menu. I proudly presented this menu and couldn't understand the audacity of this teacher condemning it. She read it to the class as an example of how a menu should not be written.

The atmosphere at the restaurant was always loud and adversarial, with the main topic always being cricket and politics. My stepfather and his brother always supported the other side while most of the patrons were always avid supporters of the West Indies Cricket Team. There was always a difference when it came to politics.

As a child I used to look at the layout of the restaurant and wonder what improvements could be made. For instance, the heavy, colored, plastic table cloths; the heavy, aluminum eating spoons, and the bottled pepper sauce, were all changes I thought would be made when I opened my own restaurant.

An incident occurred one day that embarrassed me and, for the most part, the entire family. One day as I was approaching the restaurant, I saw a large crowd gathered and on listening carefully, I recognized my mother's voice in high octave. As I drew closer, I saw my two brothers sitting barefooted and my mother in the food preparation area shouting at my stepfather. My uncle was having none of this in his place and was reminding his brother that this woman was the wrong fit as evident by the embarrassment she was causing him. It was when my stepfather decided he would ignore her and get on with his work that my mother decided to scramble him. To this my stepdad reacted by slamming her to the ground.

There was mayhem on Mucurapo Street because Dootsy started to shout, "Murder! Police! This man killing me!" They had to lift her up and put her in a taxi to take her to the nearby hospital. It didn't stop there because the driver decided he would wait to get other passengers. My mother kept on screaming. My school mates on their way back to school were stopping and looking into the car to get the story from me. The only thing I could have done was cry. When my mother went to the hospital she got immediate attention because she never stopped screaming. Her leg was bandaged, and she was sent home.

My embarrassment continued because the next day the rumor was that my mother had taken money from a young man, and he had broken her legs. I was at pains to explain to my teachers what actually had happened. Whenever my mother had reason to seek medical attention in the hospital, I hated to be the one going with her because as she got there, whether her case was critical or not, she would make so much noise that she would get immediate attention.

Mr. Theo stopped my mother from working and so once again she was a full-time housewife. Ma loved to plant her own vegetables, so she made use of the extra land to plant., Coming from the country, Ma planted mostly the crops she knew. There were lots of peppers, so much so that the Indian neighbors came to my mother to buy peppers. She planted all the varieties of bhagi: poi, dasheen bush bhagi, Morai bhagi, and seim beans (similar to string beans). In addition, she had a huge chalta tree, the fruit from which she used to sell, or sometimes make her own amchar.

Ma could speak Patois and Hindi. She had old Indian friends that she conversed with only in Hindi. She, like my stepmother, was a very good cook, and specialized in Indian cooking. She made all the variety of rotis, as well as kuchela and amchar—the one where you dry the mangoes in the sun to absorb the oils, etc. I remember one day Ma gave me a lot of produce from her garden to take to my teacher. I was so embarrassed that I dropped them on the roadside, thinking my teacher would not appreciate it. When I got home, and she asked about my teacher's response, I told her she was happy.

Ma's perception of bringing up girls was far different from my father's. Dad's plan was that we become a teacher, a nurse or work in the Red House; while Ma always hoped that we would aim towards finding someone to marry and have children. She would often point to all her nieces who were married young and had children.

A good example of this was when Ray, a young man in the district asked me to marry him. I was only 15. I was in Form 3; marriage was the farthest thing from my mind. He wanted to approach my father, but I told him that was not a good idea, knowing my father's temperament. In addition, I looked at the old-fashioned, brown, hard khaki pants he used to wear and told myself there was no way I was going to be ironing those all the days of my life. He decided to approach my mother on the matter. This pleased her so much that she told him that the courts had given her custody over us, and she could give him the permission he needed. At that stage I knew my mother was playing with her life because my father, after spending money to educate us, was not going to allow anybody to get in the midst of his plans.

Ma eventually got married to Mr. Theophilus and became Mrs. Prime. According to her, Mr. Prime never knew she had three sons before she met him, and she would only let him know after she had married him. So, whenever my brother, Joseph, came to visit her, he had to leave before Mr. Theophilus came home.

My mother was short, about 4ft 8 inches and so she wore very high heels. She looked different from me, so when we were out together, nobody believed she was my mother. At one point, when I went to live with her, she enrolled me in a school in San Fernando. I remember one day I misbehaved in school and was told to return with my mother. My principal treated parents visiting her according to how they looked. My mother sewed her own clothes and that day, Dootsy took her time to dress. She wore a sky blue taffeta dress, cut on the A-line, with a see-through nylon top cut above the bust. She wore matching high heels. Her hair was done in a fancy Lana Turner twist, complete with a pair of attractive dark shades.

I was proud to announce to my friends that she was my mother. But alas, no one believed! I remember my friend, Patricia, telling me my mother was the maid, working for some woman, and this woman had come on my mother's behalf.

Ma found that I resembled my father, so she made my life with her a living hell. I suffered a lot of beatings from my mother for crimes I did not commit; like the time she said I had stolen her make up. I was beaten so badly with a plastic belt and told not to return home until the make-up was found. That evening, I walked miles on the train line to get home. When I got home, I remained outside, too frightened to go inside. I later found out from my little brother that she had found her make up.

One day, my teacher took me to the principal to have him look at my skin because I had gone to school that morning with welts all over my body from a beating. The evening before, Ma was moulding trees in her garden and must have accidentally damaged the roots. I was accused of doing that damage and was beaten mercilessly with a guava whip.

Each morning my task was to bathe and prepare my two brothers for school. I had to visit the nearby bakery and then make them breakfast. When they were ready, they would go downstairs to their father's car to be taken to school. When I was finished, I would then have to dress myself and then walk the very same distance to my school. My school and my brothers' school were on the same street. They were going to San Fernando Boys R.C. and I was going to San Fernando Girls E.C.

When I was about fourteen, there was an incident on Christmas Eve night when Ma said I had hidden her curtain rods, which she was about to use. Despite my denial, my mother took a machine strap and beat me so badly that all my neighbors and friends heard. I remember one of my cousins, while spending vacation with us, witnessed some of the beatings and was so petrified that she asked my mother to take her back home.

"Ignorance always impedes progress
Education saves you much distress
So learn, learn, learn, as much as you can
For the nation's future is in your hand."
Education a Must, Slinger Francisco (Mighty Sparrow)

CHAPTER 6
SCHOOLS

I attended Todd's Road R.C. School for a short time while staying with my grandmother. I remember the school was just a few yards from my uncle's house. My class was situated close to a window where I could see my aunt plying her trade outside.

My second school was Chaguanas Government. Our commute to school was on the train line. One rule my parents taught us was that we were never to accept sweets from strangers along the way. One day outside the school, two gentlemen, one black and one white, were motioning us to their vehicle, while holding sweets in their hands. Just as I was about to go towards them, my sister pulled my hand away and started running from them. We ran along the train line and never stopped until we got home.

My third school was Ecclesville E.C., where I spent the longest period, from age five to eleven. Ecclesville was in the Williamsville area and within that area, we lived a number of places. Firstly, we lived in Farnum; this is when I first met my stepmother. Following this, we moved to Hardbargain, into an old almost abandoned rented house with a broken step, and a large pomerac tree in the front yard.

At one point I attended Mt. Moriah Methodist School. I don't remember under what circumstances or at what age, but I remember the hill being high and the difficulty we suffered in coming down the hill especially when it rained. We had two choices--either crossing a muddy footpath or a steep, slippery hill--neither of which suited a small child.

Our next move was to Piparo, in another old, rented house. We loved this location because this house was built on a large parcel of land with several fruit trees. We did not own the property, but we had access to all the fruit trees. There were several varieties of mangoes, two plum trees, a sapodilla tree, a pommecythere tree and various orange trees. It was a long commute to school, and we lived a distance away from many of the students, so no one knew how poor we were.

While living in the Williamsville area, we had a problem. Most of the families in this area had houses and land of their own. We were basically looked down upon, having come as strangers into the area, living with our father in rented old houses, moving from area to area.

The last place we lived in Williamsville was in Ecclesville, obliquely opposite our school. We hated that move because now we were living close to the school where all our poverty was exposed. Here, our rent was also $3.00 per month. At the start of the month when my father couldn't pay, the landlady would create a loud scene, asking that we vacate her premises.

It was while living in the Williamsville area that I met Mr. Dookhan, who inspired me to plant my own home vegetable garden. He lived in Farnum, a predominantly East Indian area, where he grew a small vegetable garden, which he worked on mornings. On afternoons he would ride through Hardbargain—a predominantly black area, selling his produce: bodi, melongene, spinach, ochroes, etc., which most times we couldn't even afford to buy. I admired Mr. Dookhan and thought I could do what he did, utilizing every inch of unused land.

Without even getting permission from the landlord, I proceeded to erect my own "machan" made of bamboo and began planting my own seim and bodi. From there I added other crops. At one point, with the help of my dad, I planted corn on two lots of land. I must admit, planting corn was something I personally liked to do. In fact, the corn and other crops not only filled a gap, food-wise, but I was able to sell some in a nearby shop, the proceeds from which helped us many days to get money to pay for transportation.

Planting, with my Dad in front digging the holes with his hoe and me and my sister following placing the grains in the holes and covering them up, was more fun than work. We loved when it was time to reap because not only did we benefit from selling some of the crop, but our teachers benefited too.

On afternoons we would light our coal pots and have fresh roasted corn as part of our dinner. The next morning, we would either boil some or roast some, depending on the taste of those teachers we planned to give corn to. I remember one teacher would be on the chalk board with chalk in one hand and roasted corn in the other. One morning I tried to explain to Mr. Patrick, one of our teachers, that the corn could no longer be roasted because they had gotten too hard. According to him, this was no reason for him not to be enjoying some corn, because the corn could now be parched, and that would suit him just fine.

Another bi-product of the dry corn was "chili bibi". This was a snack enjoyed by children (and many adults, too). It was made by first parching the corn which was then ground with sugar and made into a tasty snack which resembled finely ground bread crumbs.

That wasn't the end of the corn season because Dad made some of the most tasty "paime" (a dish similar to tamale). Paime was made of grated corn and coconut, raisins, sugar, cinnamon and other spices, wrapped and cooked in green banana leaves. In addition, we used the corn meal to make dumplings and bakes. At the end of the season, Dad would have us put some corn to dry in readiness for the next planting season.

I left Ecclesville E.C. School at age 11 to live with my mother in Marabella. I was happy to leave because the next step for me was the Exhibition Class. I dreaded going into that class because the class teacher was Mr. Harriet. Mr. Harriet's method of punishment was beating his students behind the neck with a tamarind whip.

From there, I went to San Fernando Girls E.C. which was approximately three miles from my mother's home in Marabella. The school was situated on Harris Promenade in the same location as the Anglican Church. This school was a far cry from the one at Ecclesville. Most of the children were from families belonging to San Fernando's middle class, so I had a lot of adjustments to make in relating to them. Fighting was not allowed. Proper language was spoken. Occasionally, we were given a lecture on deportment. We were told how to keep our fingernails well-manicured; and how to ensure our socks and shoes were clean and well-polished every morning.

This, of course, was a far cry from Ecclesville, where we went to school without shoes. The only people there with shoes on were the principal's children. Some of the well-known names in San Fernando Girls School were the Granderson sisters, the McLears, the De Gannes, the Coelhos, the Woodings, and the Leungs; these names all told a story of affluence and influence.

San Fernando Girls E.C. transformed my life in that I was exposed to a completely different way of thinking. Those occasional lectures by one of the teachers, Ms. Popplewell, taught me how to have purpose in my life. It was after one of her lectures that I decided I wanted to go to secondary school. That day I told my mother my plans. She did not like the idea. Instead, she said she had already made plans for me to attend a sewing class, but I took it upon myself to obtain forms for a secondary school. This landed me in trouble with my mother, because she packed my bags and posted me back to my father's.

Ecclesville

So, there I was back at Ecclesville E.C. School, now aged 13. My dad didn't just ask for me to be re-admitted but he insisted that he had to visit the home of the principal and explain his whole life story involving his ex-wife and how he came to be in charge of us, and he did this all within the hearing of the principal's children! My new refined appearance and habits, my long-manicured nails didn't sit kindly with the principal, and he immediately ordered that I cut them. I was laughed at and mocked, with the children calling me "Socks and Shoes" because now I was looking much more refined; no longer attending school without shoes. I now owned lily-white crepe-soles and matching white socks.

Children provoked me in a number of ways to fight, because in order to survive in that school, you had to be able to fight. In fact, you gained a lot of respect when you were a good fighter. So being away for so long I had lost my skills. You can imagine my joy when the term ended, and I was accepted into Excelsior High School.

Everybody had a nick name which you lived with all your school life. My nick name was "Bungles", because during the recitation of a poem I mispronounced 'bugles' and said 'bungles' because I copied it wrong, so I had to live with the name. Fighting was so real in this school that even the teachers did not escape. There was a teacher whose nick name was Five Dollars. There was no explanation as to why she got the name. They would block her car after school shouting her nick name and making it difficult for her to drive. At one point she was even prevented from entering her car and had to get the assistance of other male teachers.

Our pastime after school was either to have fights or call out some neighbor with an impediment and make fun of him or her. If that person would attempt to answer, they would become the butt of our jokes. For example, Mr. Clunis had one eye, so we made up a song on him and taunted him each afternoon.

On our way from school, we had to greet all the villagers whether they were outdoors or indoors. So, children would call the name of these villagers, such as Ms. Sill and she would shout back her loud response. The neighbors would look forward to our dismissal from school each day to hear from the children. I remember when I got to the Allahars, who were Muslim, to shout, *Salaam u alaikum,* and they would answer, *Alaikum salaam.*

The one thing I absolutely hated about the school at Ecclesville was the fact that each morning we had to go into the bushes behind the school yard and cut branches to sweep the dusty dirt yard. Imagine a situation where you already had no shoes on and having to sweep and clean all the dust from the previous day! Such was life in a country school, but no parent complained.

My father had an older girl take us to school when I was five and my sister was three. Her name was Claudine. She had an older brother whose name was Errol. She became somewhat of a big sister to us. We got some respect when people found out that we had an 'older' sister. My sister and I had book bags made from empty flour bags. My sister's bag had her name written on it: "Ola". One day Claudine placed her books in my sister's bag. When we got to school, we found twelve cents in the bag. Not knowing where the money had come from, we spent it. We bought bread and channa, sugar cakes, soft drinks, etc.

We were so excited about our good fortune that we told Claudine about it. Apparently, her grandmother had given her the money to buy soap in the village. When she put her books in Ola's bag the money had dropped in. She thought she was in trouble for having lost the money, so she was happy to put us in the firing line. My poor dad did not have the money to give back, and had to wait until he received his next pay packet.

Most days coming home from school, Claudine would have her friends, Shirley and Chinee come over. Whenever they spoke around us, they would speak a secret language 'gibberish' (a made up language like pig latin). I silently vowed that one day I would be able to speak that language too. Even to this day, whenever traveling among people who spoke several languages, my husband and I would use it as our secret second language.

Some of the infant classes had to be housed in the church which is where my sister was. It took almost a whole term before teachers realized that my sister Earla would spend her days under the church building, playing and sleeping in the dirt. That same Earla remained in that school all her primary school days, achieving trophies in long distance running for the school, taking leading roles in all school activities, and always being at the head of the class.

The Ecclesville school always had a robust kitchen garden with sweet peppers, lettuce, patchoi, celery. The villagers didn't know how to use a lot of these vegetables, so the principal was happy to take them home.

Children came from the various little villages around which were noted for different kinds of fruit. The village of Poona was famous for "Banga" (gru gru boef). Whiteland was famous for cerises. The Guaracara Road leading to Farnum was famous for tonca beans. Ecclesville had a lot of citrus plantations. On our way home, we often visited some of these places getting into trouble by venturing into somebody's property to help ourselves to some of their fruit.

Secondary School

My secondary school life was bittersweet. We lived with our father during this time in Piparo, which was approximately six miles from San Fernando, where my school was situated. Our commute to school was in an old Rambler car driven by my father's Muslim friend. He actually was trying to help my father because he was in a similar situation, having lost his wife. So daily we were cramped into this car—six boys in the back and three girls in the front seat. When we arrived on the promenade, we would walk for another two miles up Mt. Moriah Hill to our school, often dripping wet when we got there.

Our school did not have a science lab. I guess this was the case with a lot of the private secondary schools in San Fernando. In my day, there were only four so-called prestigious secondary schools in San Fernando. There was the Exhibition exam, and this entitled only about five or six children from each primary school entry into these schools. The rest of us went to private schools, where we had to pay for our tuition. Very often parents were delinquent in paying our fees. Thankfully, while the principal would send children who owed fees back home, he never sent us. This was because Dad always kept in touch with the principal, so he knew of our plight.

I did very well in school. I hated algebra and geometry, but my arithmetic was good. My writing and oratory skills and language were good. We used to have morning service before the start of each day. I remember as a Form Three student seeing Form Five students and also teachers conducting morning worship poorly. So, on one occasion I asked the principal to allow me to do the honors. That morning after getting on stage with Bible passage in hand, I conducted the morning's service, holding everybody's attention from start to finish. From that day my popularity soared.

Throughout my secondary school life, my dad didn't buy me textbooks. I used my sister's books or borrowed books from friends. We didn't have electricity in our area, so we studied with lamps or sometimes with a flambeau.

In private secondary school, we were short-changed in that most teachers were not trained or qualified. Most of them had just had a 3rd grade education or maybe a grade 2. The smart ones who graduated from the prestigious schools stayed with us for maybe a term or two. I remember each time we got a good teacher, we would rejoice. Just before the final examination, our French teacher left us for a more lucrative job. Our principal could not source another French teacher so I decided that since I knew the basics, I would memorize the whole French dictionary—I had to pass that exam! On the day of the oral examination, the examiner, who was French, conducted the exam speaking real French while we were accustomed to teachers who always mispronounced. You could imagine when on the morning of my oral exam, the examiner started to speak real French, I was totally lost. Qualified teachers accepted the job just as a stepping stone to their real calling.

There was a day when after reading my essay for the class, one of my classmates insisted that she had read this story in a book. The teacher for a while believed her. It was only after other teachers told him of my writing ability did he believe that I was the writer.

Students attending our school came from surrounding areas

including Princes Town, Fyzabad, Point Fortin, and Claxton Bay. We were happy that no one lived in our area, so no one knew about our way of life. I remember the day Lyn came to our school. She was the first person from our area to attend our school. She didn't hesitate to let others know that my father was the village drunk and we were very poor.

Our school was predominantly East Indian. Most of the teachers didn't care about your ethnicity as long as you excelled. There was, however, one teacher who, I remember up to this date, would behave as though we never existed. I see him around even today, standing out in society and I remember him for the racist that he was. My sister Ruby was in a higher form and didn't do very well academically, so teachers would often make comparisons between us. This constant comparison had an adverse effect on her.

Nearing the examination period, all our hopes were squashed when Ruby suffered a nervous breakdown and decided she would drop out of school. This was a hard blow because my father was nearing retirement and we had hopes that my sister would graduate and maybe get a job and lift the burden from our father.

At this point, my younger sister, Earla, graduated from primary school. She was 14 years old, and the principal was reluctant to admit her. Even though he eventually did, we didn't know how her fees were going to be paid. In the end, all three of us managed to attend secondary school.

During the summer vacation some of my friends were fortunate to obtain jobs in some retail stores in San Fernando. Because it was important that my sister and I find some means of getting an income, I decided to approach a garment factory in the Marabella area which was recruiting sales persons to market their clothing. This business involved making and wholesaling children's garments. I don't know whether it was my youth or my willingness to work that endeared me to them, but I was given the opportunity to sell some of their clothing.

Feeling very excited about my first job as a sales person for this small garment factory, I began my morning walk from house to house with my red bag in hand, filled with some of the most beautiful, locally made children's dresses. I remember going into an area on the Bye Pass, called St Joseph Village, where a lot of foreigners lived. The first person to show interest was a young white girl who apparently lived with her father, an expatriate employed with the Pointe a Pierre refinery.

Apart from liking the dresses, she was happy to converse with another young person. In the end she asked that I return another day when her father would be home. On my return, her father anxious to please his daughter, purchased two of the dresses.

This first sale increased my appetite for the job. I went to visit different areas on alternate days. Some days didn't always go well. Sometimes, I met rude and disrespectful people and ferocious dogs, but at the end of the day something would happen to give me encouragement. There was this day when a shower came down while I was in an area with high walls and locked gates. In attempting to get to a shelter, I was faced with a huge drain filled with water. That day I was watersoaked, but fortunately my bag was intact.

At the end of the period, I was feeling proud of myself that I was able to make a contribution to improve our financial situation.

I must mention our two Chinese friends, Sylvia and Stella Wooling The Woolings came from a similar domestic background as we did. Their father had come from China and worked in a Chinese restaurant. They lived somewhere in the countryside, and stayed in a little back room to be close to school. They befriended us because we had the same drive to succeed. Their father couldn't speak a word of English, but he acknowledged us as his daughters' friends. Many evenings when our driver failed to pick us up, this old Chinese man would look and see us marooned, motion to us to come across and give us taxi fare, enough to take us home. All the while my stepfather, who would be plying his trade in a nearby taxi stand, would ignore us. I wish I could see my friends today to tell them thanks.

Home to me is many places
Cause many places is where I have lived
Many places is where I have learned and grown.
Home Is Many Places, Keisha Oleaga

CHAPTER 7
PLACES LIVED

My parents constantly fought over us. This resulted in their stealing us and hiding us from each other. Even though the courts granted Ma custody of us, my father decided he would fight on his own to parent us. This meant that we lived several places in Trinidad — some long-term, some short term.

My sisters and I were born in Chaguanas, where we lived for a short time with both parents. After their falling out, we lived in Todd's Road with our grandma. People often ask me how I remember some incidents. One thing I do remember is the taste of the bitter asafetida my mother rubbed on her breasts to prevent us from breast feeding. This occurred while we were in Chaguanas. From there we went to Williamsville. While in Williamsville we moved from Farnum to Hardbargain, then to Piparo, then to Ecclesville. I personally spent some time with my mother in Marabella.

During the short time we spent in Barrackpore with some of my mother's family, hidden away from Dad, I remember my ears being pierced by a cousin, May, who was much older than us and had just learned the technique. This resulted in my ears being pierced in the wrong place—I had to live with this for the rest of my life.

Barrackpore was a very rural town in those days where accessibility to hospitals, doctors, etc., was limited. Once, after a nightfall of rain, the ground was damp and soggy. I observed a pretty colored bracelet resting under some leaves. Motioning to my sister, I approached it. My cousin May who happened to look outside, screamed at us to move away. It was only later that we found out that the pretty bracelet was a deadly coral snake!

I remember staying in Laventille by some of my father's family. I don't remember what part of Laventille it was, but I remember the house was on a hill, and at mealtimes we would walk down the hill to go by another member of the family. The food and drinks were served in calabash bowls. Up to today I can taste that mauby drink they served us.

Some aspects of life in Marabella were good, in that Ma lived in a somewhat new house with all the amenities of the day. She had all the things we did not have while we were living with my dad, such as a refrigerator, a gas stove with an oven, and she even had Morris chairs, which were popular in those days. There was also a dining room set, a television; and things that made life comfortable, like running water. We were also in close proximity to shops, parlors, markets, and even a cinema. In Marabella, I had my own circle of friends, most of whom were from nearby schools in San Fernando.

My mother had done pretty well for herself. She had married again, had two boys for her new husband and owned this new house in Marabella. Living in Marabella, we were close to the train line and even the ocean. Many days we would walk down to the beach for a swim or even to catch Waco, a small shellfish. One day after cooking and not cleaning this fish properly, we all got sick and had to get medication. Because of our closeness to the river and the sea, my brothers often made traps for catching crabs. There was a river at the back of where we lived which I guess was the Guaracara River. It separated Gopaul Lands from the other residents whom my mother often described as people from the other islands.

The popular betting game in Marabella was Whe Whe. It was illegal, but almost the whole area participated. This was a form of gambling that provided a livelihood for many. My uncle, my stepfather's brother, was one of the people who visited homes each afternoon to collect their bets to take to the "banker". The banker was the person who decided which number played for the day. Each number represented a symbol. I remember 5 was priest, 29 was obeah man, 9 was cattle, etc. People looked for every sign to decide what the banker would play on any given day.

My mother used to fill a tumbler of water, place it on a flat surface and light a match on the water. She would get a formation. They would stare into the glass for hours trying to fathom what was the formation. One day I looked into the glass and told them it looked like a yard fowl. They all dismissed me and went on with their own findings. That day when the winning number was declared: it was 26, fowl. Everybody was disappointed because nobody played my number. From that day, my mother always called on me to look into the glass and determine the symbol.

We lived in so many places, it is difficult to remember where we lived and our ages at any given time. For instance, there was a time when I was about seven, staying with my mother on Coffee Street in San Fernando. The rented apartment was opposite Mc Enearney Car Sales. I remember looking out at the young ladies who worked there, all nicely dressed, wearing their high heels and their hobble skirts. They were all white and I thought that this was the norm in all motor car companies.

One day, my mother went out to work selling her sweepstake tickets. There was an empty drum at the back of our house. After playing with the drum for some time, my sister and I both fell into it. It was only when the drum fell and started to roll that we realized that we were stuck and couldn't get out. The drum kept rolling back and forth. Luckily for us, according to my mother, there was no rain that day. We had to remain stuck until my mother returned home.

We had to move from that location in a hurry when my mother realized that Dad was in the area looking for us. We moved again to Navet, where Ma opened a small parlor. One day, Ma went out and closed up the parlor and left us inside. That day we drank as many soft drinks as our little stomachs could take. We ate about the same number of sweets. My mother's form of punishment was to use a celluloid belt on us. That day she used the belt on all of us. I don't recall whether I was the ringleader, but I was held by the hair, knocked against the counter of the parlor and got a large cut above my eye. I have the scar up to this day.

I don't remember how much back-and-forth my parents had before the courts awarded custody to my mother. It was only after an agreement was made between her and Dad that he could have us that we had some stability in our lives. We were given to our dad with the understanding that we would be allowed to visit Ma from time to time.

The President of the Single Father's Association at that time, always reminds me of my father in the way he has fought the courts for custody of his son, because like my father he believed he would make a better parent. In retrospect, my father was indeed the better parent, because for the most part he was responsible for making us successful adults. His aim and desire for us was far greater than my mother's.

"Remember not the sins of my youth,
nor my transgressions:
according to thy mercy, remember thou me
for thy goodness sake, O Lord."
Psalm 25:7

CHAPTER 8
FINDING A WAY

Throughout my life I have always found a way to get things done. I will lay out the facts and let you be the judge.

One night, while we three girls were staying with my mother, our friends in the area were having a party. When we asked Ma for permission she told us we could go, providing we came home before six. The party's starting time, however, was 8.00 P.M. That day I assured them I would find a way for us to attend the party. That night we went to bed early and when we thought everybody was asleep, I took pillows and made 'mummies' on the bed, sneaked out through the front door and went to the party.

Throughout the night we were constantly looking at the door whenever we heard a noise, expecting anytime Ma would come and drag us outside. Our plan included leaving our night clothes downstairs, and in case we were found out, our excuse would be that we heard a noise and went downstairs to investigate. Everything was well planned and executed. We had pulled it off!

When my mother's birthday was approaching I went to Woolworth's, a popular store at that time, and bought her a jar of hair cream. Ma was pleased with her gift and asked me the price. Actually, the grease cost 27 cents but I didn't want her to think it was too cheap, so I told her it cost 54 cents. Every time the jar was empty she would ask me to get her another, each time earning for myself 27 cents. I paid a heavy price the day my mother went to Woolworth's herself and discovered the price was actually 27 cents!

Now, living with my father was no bed of roses either. At the end of the year when my father would get his bonus he would shop for his three girls. Dad's shopping meant he would buy yards of patterned cloth that he would take to the seamstress to make dresses, half-slips and panties for all of us out of the same material. Also, when dad received his money he would spend out of it on drinks with his friends. Very often he would ask me to check his balance to see how much he still had. One day I told him there was less than the case, and when he believed me, my sisters and I were able to do some shopping for ourselves, buying panties, half-slips, bras, etc. When dad asked where we got those things, we told him from our mother.

While living with my mother, I used to ask permission to go to church on Sundays, mainly because our school was in the Anglican Church yard, and I knew most of the children in the Sunday school. Also, Auntie Kay's children's talent show used to be held in the Empire Cinema a few yards away from the church. So many Sundays, instead of going directly to church I would go to Auntie Kay's show. One Sunday I knew my mother would ask me about the sermon, so I decided I would go to the late service so I would have something to tell her. I was pleasantly surprised to find myself sitting in the middle of a church full of foreigners complete with their own foreign priest. The following day I found out that the expatriates in Point-a-Pierre had their own service, conducted by their own priest, and it took place at a later time.

A sibling is the lens through
which you see your childhood.
Ann Hood

CHAPTER 9
MY SIBLINGS

My mother had eight children: five boys and three girls. Three of the boys she had early in life before she had met my father. She then married my father and had us three girls. After divorcing my father, she married my stepfather and had two boys. The three older boys we never knew until late in life. We just knew of them. However, one of them, Joseph, went on to play a most important role in our lives.

My two younger brothers, Conrad and Junior, were the sons of my mother's latest husband and they meant the world to her. Conrad was the quiet one, and good with his hands. All the young boys in the area would gather under my mother's house to have him make their kites. A "mad bull" kite from Conrad was always a winner. He was good at making skateboards, wooden canal carts, etc.

The younger one was my mother's favorite. He was the one who got the best toys but would be the first to damage them. He would blame us for damaging his toys and this would make our mother pack our bags and send us back to our father. This often took place around Christmas when we had nothing to go back to. We often got the impression that my brother would be encouraged to insist that we damaged his toys so our mother would have an excuse to get rid of us. Those were terrible times because Dad was never in a position to celebrate Christmas, so we would spend the entire season locked away in the house because we never wanted the neighbors to know we were back home.

Our two brothers were taught to treat us badly, to disrespect us and very often to let us know that we were not welcome in their house. Our brothers knew nothing about us except for those times that we would spend with them. To them, we weren't important; they didn't know where we lived, neither did they care. At one point, they both got bicycles as Christmas gifts and started to race as a hobby. Junior, my younger brother, eventually passed the exam for St. Benedict's College and made a lot of friends who were also cyclists.

When my brothers reached the age of 13 and 15, they realized that we were no longer visiting my Mom because we had left to live with my brother, Joseph. They wanted answers from my mother which apparently were not forthcoming. One morning, they took their bicycles and rode from Marabella in search of us. We were happy to see them and the questions they wanted answers to were about our background: Why were we treated so badly by my mother? Where did we live and under what conditions, and why were we now living by my brother in Tunapuna? That morning, I saw my brothers cry when we told the story of our lives. My younger brother resolved that he would return home and confront my mother.

One can understand how I felt when the following week, on a Wednesday to be exact, I found out that my beloved brother, Junior, had died in a car accident. I mourned his death for a whole year. I lost a lot of weight and even today when I see a young man with a slight resemblance of him I would agonize.

After Junior's death, nothing in the Prime home was the same. Ma died at age 56 because of uncontrolled diabetes; her husband died two years later. My brother, Conrad, tried to get on with his life after the loss of his parents and his brother. After a time, he himself got tired and ended up in the St Vincent de Paul home for the poor. He eventually got a stroke and died, but the story of how he lost my mother's property was never told to us.

My Sister Earla

When Ruby and I left to live with our brother, Joseph, we left our little sister Earla with our mother. The aim was to have her finish school and then send for her. As soon as she finished school she started to live with us. To avoid depending on our brother, she took a job in St James, taking care of a baby. Earla had a sleep walking problem though. She was required to be on the job for 7.00 a.m.; however, on more than one occasion she found herself at the bus station at 1.00 a.m. We had a lot of problems dealing with this situation on our own.

My sister always had a short temper and because our characters differed, she and I always crossed swords. She was a cross every T and dot every I kind of person, whereas I was just the opposite. Interfering with her things would always result in a fight. There was a day she came home and found out that I had interfered with her things; it resulted in a big fight. We crossed paths while she was ironing, and she attempted to brand me with the iron. My friend, whose house I ran to for protection, ridiculed me for running. I had to explain that I knew my sister would not have put the iron down until she had branded me. I was protecting myself.

I was ecstatic the day I found out that she was accepted into Connaught Hospital in the UK. The problem arose when my brother and I realized that we didn't have the funds to assist her. Even though we got loans from family and friends to help, it still was not enough and Earla left for London with a light suitcase. She had absolutely no warm clothes and she was leaving during the winter period; so we knew she was going to have a problem. I remember looking at the aircraft as it disappeared into the sky and going home and crying myself to sleep.

Phones weren't readily accessible during those days, so she wrote occasionally, but it took approximately eight years before we were able to hear her voice. She told us of all the hardship she had encountered during her early years. I always felt that my little sister was my responsibility, so I made her success in a foreign country my business. Earla was so aware of this that it took her about seven years before she could tell me that she had gotten pregnant as soon as she arrived in England, and had a son.

Earla subsequently got married and had a daughter. Imagine our delight when my husband and I were able to go to England for the first time to visit her, her new husband, my nephew and my niece. This was an entire month of celebration, reliving all our old stories.

As three girls growing up with my father, he always defined our roles. My eldest sister Ruby always did the laundry, my sister Earla was so good at cleaning that he put her in charge of that. She was so good at it that she was nicknamed "The Royal Packer". Me, I was in charge of the cooking. I was good at taking the little we had and making it into a sumptuous dish. It is no wonder that on all our visits to her home in England she would clean and do laundry and I would take charge of the kitchen. I loved to visit Walthamstow market and witness all the English vendors advertising their ground provisions, calling them by strange names.

It was indeed a game-changer when we realized that there were deceptive people all over the world. We spent a lot of money buying from young men selling 'brand name' perfumes on the street and even giving out samples. We bought several bottles for ourselves and also as gifts, only to realize they were all counterfeit. We got scammed so often at daily auctions that my sister forbade us from attending them.

I stopped on the street one day by this blond, blue-eyed fortune teller. I was always in the habit of not wearing my wedding ring. So, we had a good laugh when this lady told me that I wanted to get married to the young man that was standing close to me and she would conduct her spell for him to do so.

I felt that I didn't spend enough time with my sister before she contracted a terrible cough and became quite ill. Even though she lived in England, worked in a hospital and had the best health care, she wasn't able to combat the problem. She eventually died at age 46.

When my niece and nephew came to Trinidad, we would often take them to visit the countryside and some of our old friends. My nephew, Damian, at age seven went to school with my brother-in-law, Charles. He was asked to tell the students about life in England. We were all so proud when like a typical English boy he was able to explain all about the weaknesses of Margaret Thatcher's policies. He was so good that he was asked to visit another day. His sister, Erica, went to school in Trinidad with my children for a little while. She, on the other hand, was very shy and had a problem adjusting.

"A brother is born to help in time of need."
Proverbs 17:17b

Me at age 16 - standing outside my mother's house

My first office job

Executive secretary class of 1972

Avocado restaurant opening

My Older Brother

My younger sister in her nurse's uniform in England

My mother, Novelyia- better known as Lucy

My husband – my soulmate

My older sister, lending assistance at the start of the new business- 1981

My 70th birthday party with family members

A picture of me at my 70th birthday party

My two lovely and accomplished daughters

Meeting Joel Osteen at Lakewood church in Houston

Excited to meet Pastor Benny Hinn

PART II

CHAPTER 10
CONFRONTING THE CHALLENGES

After Dad lost his job I saw trouble on the horizon. Dad had no savings, and absolutely no means of supporting us. We were not able to pay our rent, which was only $3.00 per month. There was a neighbor who did her cooking outdoors. We would check to see when she would be finished and go over knowing that she would offer us a plate. Instead of eating it on spot, we would take it home to divide among all of us. For dinner we would often go back to the neighbor's. This time she would invite us upstairs for dinner.

These people were Seventh Day Adventists, and I am not sure whether they realized what we were going through but they placed huge plates of food before us. I remember one night we were so hungry, we grabbed the bakes and started to eat before they had begun to pray. For a while we wondered why dad had brought us to this place because in the former place, Piparo, at least we had access to fruits. Here in Ecclesville we had to purchase everything, and we had no money.

Dad was now 60 years old, and retired from his job in the quarry. My older sister now 19, also had no job. I had just turned 17 and was given a letter from Canon Farquahar to take to Coffee E.C. School. I realized that accepting a job as a pupil teacher was not going to fill the gap because we urgently needed a place to live.

At this juncture, I decided to come up with a plan of my own. My plan was to obtain a job as a live-in Nanny where I would get immediate accommodation, pay my father's rent, save some money for at least a year, and then travel to England to pursue nursing. Please note: I hated nursing! My dream was to become a radio announcer like the famous June Gonzales so that the students who shunned me in school would one day long to be my friend. At this point my plan seemed to be my only option.

I figured that I had to let someone know of our situation. My mother knew but she did nothing to help. I decided I had to do something. This is when I remembered my eldest brother, Joseph, who had a reasonable job with the Public Transport Service Corporation (PTSC). I decided to contact him and ask for his help.

With the little money Dad had gotten from the sale of our toy piano, I went by bus, in search of my brother. Sitting in the bus, I cried all the way from Marabella to Port of Spain. An elderly man sitting next to me said, "Chile, why are you crying? You are breaking my heart." I looked at him and wondered what was the point of telling him; he couldn't help. He further went on, "If you don't tell me, I wouldn't be able to help." This only helped to increase my tears.

When I got to the bus terminal in Port of Spain, it was approximately 11.00 a.m. I was thirsty and hungry. I had remained in the terminal from 11.00 a.m. to 4.00 p.m. with no sight of a Tunapuna bus.

There was this nuts vendor using all sorts of funny jokes and one-liners to sell his nuts. Around 4.00 o' clock, he came to me and said: "Chile, I notice you standing here for the entire day. Where are you going?" I told him I was going to Tunapuna. To this he replied, "You don't have to wait for a Tunapuna bus. You can take an Arouca bus, a Five Rivers bus, an Arima bus. Look, over there is an Arouca bus. Take that one." I thanked him and went on to the bus, still not sure whether he had given me the correct information.

On my way to Tunapuna, the bus stopped at Morvant, Barataria, San Juan, Mt Hope, Champs Fleurs, St. Joseph, Curepe. When I started to get concerned, I went to the driver to enquire whether this bus was going to Tunapuna. This fatherly-looking driver enquired exactly where I was going and told me to relax, he would drop me at my destination, Pentecostal Trace, Tunapuna. After making some enquiries when I alighted, I met this motherly-looking lady who showed me the little apartment where my brother lived. I sat in this lady's kitchen as she was preparing dinner and cried while relating my predicament. I was hungry and tired and was happy when this lady offered me dinner and a place to stay until my brother came. I was indeed happy to meet with my brother, whom I hardly knew.

My brother arrived around 6.00 p.m. and was both happy and surprised to see me. My brother had grown up in Mayaro and knew he had sisters, but knew very little about us. He took me into his little apartment and after all the formalities, I started to relate our plight. He was shocked to learn that we didn't grow up with my mother and that my father was the person who had raised us. I told him of my plan to help my father and my sisters to get out of the situation. The part about getting a live-in job did not sit well with him but he said this would be a last resort.

We agreed in the end that if I returned with Ruby, we should do so on a Thursday because this was his salary day. He also assured me that he was prepared to help us with accommodation, etc., until we could find jobs.

Having gone back to my father's home in Williamsville, where nothing had changed, we continued to depend on meals from the next-door neighbor. After about three weeks, and seeing no change in our circumstance, Dad suggested that I go back to my mother and explain our situation. That afternoon Ma was sitting in her front porch and as soon as she glanced through the ventilated blocks and saw me approaching, she did what she was accustomed doing: she hid all her freshly baked breads and cakes in her bedroom.

I entered the house through the back door, still smelling the aroma of what she had just baked. I explained my reason for the visit: the fact that Dad no longer worked, how we had no food and that we were totally dependent on the neighbor. This didn't seem to bother Ma; in fact, she reminded us that we were our father's responsibility and he had to find a way to provide for us.

After hearing how my mother felt, and knowing that there was nothing to go back home to, I broke down and started to cry. That day I cried so loudly that my step father entered the room and ordered me out. My younger sister, who was staying with Ma at this time (she always kept one girl to help with her work), came and consoled me. She told me that my brother had sent $20.00 for me to sign up for a subject I had to repeat. I went downstairs, washed my face, dried my tears, took a taxi and went back home to my father.

At that point I knew that $20.00 had to work for me. Back home, I told my sister I had a plan. I couldn't tell my father what had taken place at my mother's. I just told him that my brother volunteered to help us find jobs and we had plans to go to his place.

It was on a Monday when we decided to pack our bags and return to my mother's place, where we would stay until Thursday, when my brother would get paid. (It was easier to commute from Marabella, where Ma lived, to Port of Spain and thence to Tunapuna, where my brother lived). So, we planned to journey from Williamsville to Marabella, hoping to take the bus from there to Port of Spain, and then to Tunapuna.

When we arrived back at my mother's, our explanation as to why we were there was that our father had sent us. We knew that we were going to stay at her place until Thursday when we would take our bus to my brother's. Ma's response to the situation was to withhold food from us, thereby forcing us to leave. Using what was left of our $20.00, each day we would buy a quart of bread from a nearby bakery, purchase some butter, a soft drink and have a meal. It was a total surprise to my mother when Thursday arrived, and we told her we were leaving.

"Goodbye, Ma. We are leaving," I informed her.

We sounded confident, so she asked, "Where are you all going?"

Trembling, my sister said, "We are going by Joseph, Ma."

"I didn't send you all by Joseph. I sent you all by your father!"

At this point, I pulled my sister's hand and said, "I don't have the time to argue with Ma. Let's go!"

Traveling by bus this time with my sister, Ruby, I felt pretty sure of myself because I knew exactly where I was going. This time we got to the bus terminus and did exactly what the nuts vendor had told me. I took an Arima bus with the hope of arriving in Tunapuna. This time, however, on the way things looked different. I didn't see many traffic lights and the bus didn't make as many stops.

When it became obvious that something was wrong, I enquired from a young lady sitting at the back, whether the bus was indeed stopping in Tunapuna. To my surprise she pointed out that the bus was going directly to Arima passing on the highway, with limited stops. We stopped on the highway in Curepe, and walked approximately three miles to the main road. At that point we had only a few pennies from our $20.00. A kind driver eventually agreed to take what we had and drop us to Tunapuna.

My brother was very kind to us. He was excited to let everybody know that he had sisters. He introduced us to all his friends. He sent us shopping for clothes in a sale at Kirpalani's, a popular department store, so we could look presentable. We also had the experience of going to the cinema on our own to see the movie, "My Fair Lady", which was mind-boggling, to say the least. However, three of us living in my brother's one room apartment soon proved to be uncomfortable. The room was approximately 10'x10', with one front door and one window. The furniture comprised of one chair, a small bed, and a small wooden table. He had a two-burner stove on which he did his cooking.

Sometimes, my brother would work a double shift so that we could use his bed. Even though he didn't complain, we realized our search for a job and a home was not yet over; we had to move on. We were also cognizant of the fact that we were laying a heavy burden on this brother whom we hardly even knew.

We decided to register with an employment agency whose ad we found in the newspapers. The fact that we left our dad at home penniless, and at the mercy of the landlady, made it more urgent that each of us get a job to send some money back to him.

Early one morning we bade farewell to my brother, and headed to an employment agency in Port of Spain, hoping to get a placement the same day. We didn't look too bad. I was wearing a brown cotton dress, cut on the A-line, with a zipper that ran right down the front. The cost of that dress was $5.00, and because it was bought in a "buy one, get one free" sale, my sister was wearing a similar dress, but hers was grey.

When we got to the agency, we were surprised to learn that we had to pay a registration fee and present a certificate of good character before getting a job. Off we went to the police station, luggage in hand, thinking we would receive the certificate the same day. Imagine our disappointment when we learnt that we had to wait three weeks before we could get the certificate. I don't know whether the gentleman who conducted the interview saw the desperation in our young faces and our luggage, but he made an exception and gave us the certificate.

Back at the agency, I was sent to a family in Petit Valley, known as the Howard's.

"God isn't limited by where you begin.
No matter where you come from,
with God's help you can become someone
who makes a difference in this world."
Dodie Osteen

CHAPTER 11
THE HOWARDS

I left my sister at the agency and never realized where she was until a few weeks later. After I settled down at the Howards, I called the agency and found out that she had gone to a family in Diamond Vale.

My stay with the Howards gave me the opportunity to meet new people and gain some experience. Firstly, I was introduced to the maid who was about to retire. She told me she was also from the country, and that she had been working at that job for the last two years, with the hope of making enough money to study nursing in England. I told myself if she was working for two years to accumulate enough to travel to England that was definitely too much time for me to remain in this job. Immediately, I foresaw a stumbling block. She told me her paperwork was completed, her bags were packed and hence her reason for leaving. Speaking to Beryl gave me the encouragement I needed. We became friends and she was able to show me around.

The Howards lived in a very large house in Petit Valley. They owned a haberdashery store in Port of Spain which the husband managed. The wife was a stay-at-home mom who spent most of her time going to the beauty parlors, and enjoying breakfast with friends, etc. I started to call her Mrs. Howard, but she told me she preferred to be called Madam.

On mornings, I was required to wear a blue dress with an apron. My duties included making breakfast, bathing and getting the children ready for school each day. The Howards had two boys, ages five and four, and a little three-year-old girl. This was the most difficult part of the job because these boys were the most unruly children I have ever seen. While I was getting them dressed they fought, they rolled, they jumped on the beds, they ran from me. They saw laughter in everything I attempted to do. Beryl handled it well, but for me it was traumatic, and I wondered how I would cope when she was not around.

Following this, I was required to clean and vacuum this huge five-bedroom mansion, prepare lunch, and prepare for the children's return at around 3.00 p.m. I was allowed a half hour break at around 2.00 p.m. I was then to change into a white dress and apron in readiness to take the children for their afternoon walks. I told Beryl I didn't like the idea of wearing the uniform because, even though I was far from San Fernando, I couldn't risk someone seeing me dressed in a maid's uniform and walking children.

I will never forget the day while walking the children in the savannah that I came face to face with one of my primary school teachers. Ms. Hoode was the music teacher in San Fernando Girls E.C. She had probably taken her class on an outing. By the look of utter disgust on this lady's face, I knew she had instantly recognized me. I never got the chance to tell her my side of the story. After my return from the walks, I was required to prepare for Mr. Howard's return home at the end of the day. I would set the table, etc., and wait to hear his car horn, as I was required to open and close the gate.

One day, while still working at the Howards, I saw this training course being advertised for young people entering the world of work. This was a two-week afternoon training program at the Chamber of Commerce building in Port of Spain. I applied and was accepted. I asked for some time off to be able to do this course and it was granted. Throughout the course, I was admiring all those who could make a contribution to the program. Some people already had jobs and were able to make valuable contributions. Coming from the country, I felt somewhat inferior, so I said very little.

On the last day, however, we were required to do a report on the program. We were told the person with the most marks would get a job at the agency. Imagine my surprise when my name was announced as the winner. I was introduced to the Director of Liz Cromwell Employment Agency and told to report for work the following Monday.

I resigned my job at the Howard's immediately and went shopping for suitable clothes, all excited because this was going to be my first real job. I was given instructions on how to apply makeup, etc., and how to appear as a front desk person. Mrs. Howard was very disappointed when I announced my resignation, at such short notice. The next day she telephoned the same employment agency explaining her misfortune. Not for a moment did she realize she was speaking to the same Ms. Douglas who had recently resigned from her employ.

I continued speaking with Mrs. Howard for a long time, this time with my new officious voice, trying to source the right person for her job, all the while not disclosing my identity. This deception finally ended when I got someone for her, and she attempted to describe her location. I was able to tell her I knew exactly how to find her and in fact I was the same Pearl Douglas, her former employee. Needless to say, Mrs. Howard was extremely upset, not only with me, but with the entire management of the agency.

"But he knows the way that I take;
when he has tested me, I will come forth as gold."
Job 23:10

CHAPTER 12
FORGING AHEAD

I was able to obtain jobs for some of the same people who attended the training program with me. Working in that agency taught me a lot of things. For example, a number of employers specified exactly what race and color they wanted to employ. There was this employer who stated quite clearly that he wanted a very fair, mixed-race person, a fair-skinned East Indian or someone Chinese to be a salesperson. There was this guy, for instance, whom I was sending for the job, but I also planned to send another person. I don't know how he knew where I lived, but that day he came to my home to hand me an envelope with $500.00. The Lord knows I was needy, but I did not yield to temptation.

For some reason, my boss thought I was too gauche, and I needed to be more outgoing, so on afternoons, after work, she would take me to a lot of places. For the first time, I realized how much privilege a member of the press had. My boss would take me to a number of prestigious parties, and just by announcing she was a member of the press, she would get permission to enter. Working for Liz made me feel I was bigger than life because I got the opportunity to talk to her friends on the phone--all prominent people.

I remember when the now-famous Trevor Mc Dowell, whom I had gotten to know through Liz, invited me to lunch, I was so unsure of myself I didn't go. I got the opportunity to meet a lot of prominent persons, such as the Mighty Sparrow, a top calypsonian. One night after attending a show at the Penthouse, upstairs Salvatori Building in down town Port of Spain, I got the opportunity, not just to meet the Mighty Sparrow, but to sit on his lap. After the show, Liz asked Sparrow's driver to take me to the taxi stand; there was little room in the front seat, but Sparrow said I was very small and could sit on his lap. This was indeed a big occasion for me, and I could not stop talking about it.

Liz Cromwell was a popular person in the world of work. I knew very little of her credentials before I met her, but she was well-known and respected by all of her clients. She was one of the first persons in Trinidad to sport an Afro hairstyle. This she did, along with her African outfits. I remember going to Topo Carlo Restaurant with her one evening and the manager kept taunting her about her hair style and, in return, Liz was telling him about how proud she was of her identity. It was at this Italian restaurant that I tasted pizza for the first time. Liz ordered a steak and she asked that they serve me a mini pizza. I wondered what on earth that was, but I liked the taste. Pizza at that time was not popular in Trinidad, as it is today.

I lost my job with this agency in preparing my sister to come for an interview with the boss. I had seen a job opening I thought would be ideal for her. I behaved rather unprofessionally, but I was so anxious to give her the job that I gave her all the interview and exam tips. In fact, I gave her answers to all the questions. We had a proficiency test which we gave to all those seeking to obtain jobs. Candidates had to complete 50 general paper questions in a certain period. I went home and told my sister the answers to all the questions but warned her that she was not supposed to get them all correct. My sister came to the office and said everything I told her not to say. My boss realized I had prompted her, and I was fired the next day.

"Thou has turned my mourning into dancing:
thou hast put off my sackcloth,
and girded me with gladness;
To the end that my glory may sing praise to thee,
and not be silent. O Lord, my God,
I will give thanks unto thee forever."
Psalm 30:11-12

CHAPTER 13
IDC/MDC

My sister Ruby had moved away from us, by this time. My younger sister, Earla, was staying with us but her papers were being finalized to go to England. Joseph had rented a bigger apartment to accommodate all of us and as he alone was working, I felt guilty having to depend on him. I used the opportunity to attend classes at John Donaldson Technical Institute. Before the course was even completed we were advised to apply for jobs through the Statutory Authorities Service Commission (SASC).

I had bought myself a nifty three-piece suit to attend interviews. I was interviewed by both Barclays Bank, Tunapuna, and the SASC. The same week, I was offered a placement at both the bank and at the Industrial Development Corporation (I.D.C). That week I became very ill and couldn't take up either of the offers. However, my brother insisted that even though it was late I should still go in to the I.D.C. to see whether the opening was still there. My apology was accepted, and I was given the job. The I.D.C. was a company formed by the government to work under the Ministry of Industry and Commerce to develop small and medium-sized businesses. Its location was on the sixth floor of the once-famous Salvatori Building in downtown Port of Spain.

This work environment was new to me, but I met several young people who had joined around the same time. I noted, too, that the personnel manager remembered me because I had gotten two placements for her while I was working at the employment agency. The acting position I had soon came to an end and I was given another temporary position as secretary to a consultant from India, Mr. Murthi. When he was in office, Mr. Murthi would dictate a lot of reports using technical terms that I had problems transcribing; so, I was happy when that period ended, and I was given another acting appointment in the Management Development Centre.

I was to act in place of someone who had gotten into an accident. I remember going to the second floor of the building and walking along the corridor to Room 218. The Management Development Centre was also under the Ministry of Industry of Commerce. It was made up of a number of consultants, both foreign and local, with the sole objective of training and developing managerial skills in companies.

I became secretary to three local consultants and one foreign. One of my bosses used to complain that because I was young and inexperienced, I lacked the ability to provide the kind of support the department needed. One day, while discussing the training courses available for the first quarter with her foreign counterpart, she asked me the dates for the various courses. That information I was able to give her without looking at the manual. After that day, she had so much respect for me that my duties widened. I wrote the invitation letters unaided, did all the follow up, put together the final list of participants and altogether took responsibility for planning most of the training programs.

It seems that the Management Development Centre had a specially selected group of employees, possibly because the consultants had come from the International Labor Organization. Their role was to assist and train the locals, but some of the training rubbed off on us, the junior staff. Seeing that we were a training institution, we had to be precise in what we presented to the public, so M.D.C. was a great place to learn. While at John Donaldson I used to admire a certain lecturer and wished that one day I could be like her, in her language, her dress, etc. To my surprise, she became my boss at M.D.C. Incidentally, she was the founder of the National Secretaries Association; so, I happened to be in the right place at the right time.

The young lady I was acting for never returned to her job, so I continued at the M.D.C., acting in different departments and working for a number of people. I remember one day a Canadian consultant was visiting to conduct a number of problem-solving courses and I was the secretary assigned to work for him. One evening, my immediate boss—also a foreigner—invited about six of us from the department to dinner. The conversation around the table was way over my head, the foods and drinks were strange and altogether I was rather uncomfortable. When the guest of honor arrived, the Canadian consultant, I realized his wife was one of my primary school teachers from Ecclesville E.C. I introduced myself, telling her that I had attended the school where she had taught. Of course, she did not remember me, but there were some things we were able to share.

The first time I travelled outside of Trinidad was when I was given the opportunity to work in Tobago for a week. This was a general management training course with some foreign consultants and a lot of high-powered managers from Trinidad. My office manager, who was also there, was able to guide me on how to operate in a big hotel. However, she wasn't much help on the morning when I couldn't take a shower because I did not know how to open the bathroom faucet. I felt a lot better at breakfast when I overheard some of the bosses saying they had encountered the same problem.

At breakfast one morning, my boss and his friends all ordered American breakfasts with pancakes, etc. I ordered roasted bakes with cod fish buljol. My boss wanted to find out what was on my plate and when I told him, he changed his order and had everybody changing theirs. That morning, roast bakes and buljol was a hit.

When I had just started working at the M.D.C., I was perhaps the darkest person on staff. I remember the maid almost refusing to serve me coffee. Some thought I belonged to a San Fernando middle class family, and I never told them otherwise. There was this woman who always aligned me to some famous Douglases, and I never denied it. I used to keep quiet when other workers would discuss the schools they attended, the private schools their children attended, their pedigree, etc. When my mother died and we placed the notice on the radio, we dared not include the surnames of my brothers and sisters. We put only their first names. The fact that I came from a broken home and my mom had two marriages had to be kept a secret.

I took the first Executive Secretaries Program ever offered in Trinidad in 1972. This was a two-year training program offered by the Extra Mural Department. It was offered to Senior Executive Secretaries. After I applied and was accepted, I realized I was a bit outside my rank because the attendees were all very senior to me. I remember one of my colleagues from I.D.C. who was very senior to me, and an old convent girl wanted to know how I got accepted. I felt good about myself one day when the lecturer gave us a written exercise to do. I completed mine, placed it in a folder, and submitted it. The next day he came in the class asking who was Pearl Douglas. To my utter surprise, I got top marks. That took care of my insecurity. I was able to complete the course without any problems thereafter.

During my time at the M.D.C., I gained experience from a number of people. Ms. S., for instance, the secretary to the General Manager, showed me what professionalism on the job was all about. She was able to handle any situation with tact and diplomacy. As the General Manager's secretary, she understood privacy and what confidentiality was all about; you felt comfortable discussing matters of work with her. Ms. B, on the other hand, was a very stern Caucasian-looking woman with a slight foreign accent. She was in charge of the library of handouts, so it meant that consultants would write papers on various subjects, pass them to Ms. B. for final vetting and printing. She would often have exchanges with these lecturers/consultants, and would have to refer to the dictionary, and sometimes the thesaurus to determine the correct usage of a word.

My friend, Ms. O., had worked in the Centre a number of years. Her department was close to mine, so I leaned on her to get assistance on several occasions. Ms. O. was the kind of person who was versed in the Civil Service regulations, so it was foolish of me to pick a fight with her over the details of a promotion. She obviously won, and I had to apologize not only because I was wrong, but because I was fighting a strong opponent. Ms. O. became one of my best friends for years.

It was while working in the Small Business Division that I got first-hand information on how to start and manage a small business. Whenever my bosses were absent, I would have conversations with small business owners and gather important information from them. Looking at some of their balance sheets and comparing them with my net salary per month, it dawned on me that working at an eight-to-four job was not what I wanted. Of special interest to me was the person who had started a small garment factory and another who had an ice cream parlor. I realized then that it was time to resign.

Office Prayer Meetings

During my time at the M.D.C., we decided on having lunch time prayer meetings in one of the conference rooms. This was intended to win people to Jesus Christ, because while most of my colleagues belonged to some denomination, they didn't have a personal relationship with the living God and Saviour. We used to gather to share testimonies, to pray for each other, and to broaden our knowledge of God's word and the Gospel.

In this regard, we invited people from my office and others from adjoining offices in our building to attend. In addition, we got a young pastor who also was an employee from another ministry to conduct the services. We sought, and obtained, permission from our Director to use one of our conference rooms during our lunch breaks, under the condition that we kept it quiet and orderly and that we didn't exceed the one hour limit.

On one occasion, we had a visiting Israeli Pastor who told us that these lunch time office services must be conducted wisely. He admonished us to always set a good example because the eyes of the world were always on us. If we were required to stop at 1.00 p.m., at 12.45 p.m., we should be winding down. Our young pastor didn't seem to understand this, and she would often go on to 1.30 and even to 1.45 p.m. We were always warned about our timekeeping, but sadly we became complacent and often got carried away. Once when I was absent from work, an incident occurred which caused me a lot of embarrassment.

On this day, our resident pastor, Sis Molly, decided to bring a young man into the meeting who, she said, was possessed with an evil spirit. The young man's screams and the Pastor's loud commands caused people to scamper out of their offices. When I returned to work the following day, I wasn't allowed to live this down. People who were against the meetings in the first place all had their say and encouraged management to bring an end to these meetings.

We had no one to blame but ourselves for our failure to give unto Caesar the things that are Caesar's, and for our lack of good judgement. However, the time had come for me to move on, but I was glad I was able to assist in the personal, spiritual growth of some of my colleagues, even as I, too, was growing in my faith.

"You are my best friend, the father of our children,
and you are my hidden strength.
Thank you for making life so beautiful."
Betsy Farrell

CHAPTER 14
MY HUSBAND

My husband started off as my Math tutor. I had an upcoming job interview at Republic Bank and wanted to brush up on my Math. My brother remembered this lady he knew, who had two sons he felt could give me the sort of assistance I needed. The older son was approached, but he did not seem too interested. However, before he could make up his mind, the younger son volunteered.

I learnt that Cecil had just left school and was on the job market. He indicated that he could spare some time. He turned out to be the best math teacher I ever had. In fact, he made me feel that I wasn't so bad after all.

At the end of his four-week program, I felt that I had accomplished a great deal. I thanked him and thought that was the end of our acquaintance. However, after countless visits and a few dates, I realized that there was something about him that I liked. He became a casual friend, then a good friend and in the end -- my best friend.

Cecil started a job as a teacher in a primary school, and then started training at a residential Teachers' Training College. I sometimes would borrow my brother's car to visit him. Sometimes he would leave college and meet me at my work place, at the end of the day. On a rainy afternoon, we would have to make the difficult decision whether to go to the movies or go to our separate classes. The former always seemed to be the better option.

I remember the day Cecil met me downstairs Salvatori building after work had ended, to tell me he had passed his final exam and . . . we could fix a date!

That began a life filled with love, hard work and adventure with my best friend. He had all the qualities I wanted in a husband: somebody who was good with Geometry and Algebra so that when my children got to the age where they would need help he would be there; somebody who neither smoked nor drank alcohol, and who had a love for God. God alone knows who you need to walk alongside you, and who can help you fulfill God's purpose for your life.

Cecil and I got married in 1972. Our wedding took place at the prestigious Shell Savannah Club in Port of Spain. We wanted such a big wedding, and thought our parents could not manage the plans, that we did the planning ourselves.

There are two features of our wedding that we will never forget. One was the cake we chose was based on the theme of a cornucopia or "Horn of Plenty". In Trinidad, the word "horn" could have a special meaning - infidelity - and we had wanted cornucopia horns on the cake to symbolize prosperity. Cecil insisted that the horns be replaced with birds because he could just imagine his friends on seeing the cake making fun of him. The second incident worth remembering was when some of his friends from college, who when they heard he was getting married, came unannounced and made themselves comfortable. Cecil, being his usual, easy-going self, made light of the matter and made sure they were well entertained.

Our first trip together outside of the country was for our honeymoon in Grenada. When we got there, we were warned by the guest house owner that we shouldn't venture outside without first consulting him. We decided to ignore him because we wanted to have a firsthand experience of the outskirts and how the country folk lived. Having said that, we boarded a bus to take us to the far end of the country, to a village called Sauteurs. In the bus we were packed like sardines, but the driver had us sitting near to him, describing the various towns on the way.

What he failed to mention was that because it was a Thursday, activities closed after lunch.

We arrived in Sauteurs after a long and arduous drive, and being told that we couldn't get transportation back to the capital was frightening indeed. A grocer, upon hearing of our dilemma and seeing my tears, suggested that we go to another town called Grenville, or sleep in the church nearby. The drive to Grenville was another harrowing experience. We sat between loads of green bananas, a large goat with its horns poking at us as the bus went up very steep hills.

When we got to Grenville at last, there was this driver who wanted to help but all he could offer was a ride on the roof of the truck. His truck had loads of bags and his suggestion was that we lie on them for our journey back to St George's. Another man, driving an electricity truck, saw my tears and decided to drive us back to the company. From there, this kind gentleman took us in his car and dropped us back to the hotel. You can be sure that was our last venture out on our own.

Fast forward. Nine years into our marriage, I shared with my husband that I wanted to resign and open my own business. Cecil realized that this would mean that his salary would have to meet our financial commitments, until the business was established. He was always one to ensure that we had adequate insurance coverage. To give me the start I needed, Cecil took out loans, and borrowed from his parents. He had great parents who had taught him the meaning of family life and the importance of hard work.

I thank God for my husband who would listen to my crazy plans and put them into proper perspective. The only time I would get a "buff" was when I would wake him up at 3.00 a.m. to discuss another of my 'great' ideas.

Cecil rarely calls me by my name, Pearl. Whenever he called my office, he would ask for Miss Douglas. The operator would oftentimes remind him that we had no Miss Douglas on staff, but we had a Mrs. Spring. My name at home according to Cecil is still "Doug". Looking at our marriage, some people have found that we behaved like brother and sister. In fact, I often had to remind him that I was not the sister he always wanted. After 49 years, Cecil is still the best thing that has ever happened to me. "Two are better than one; because they have a good reward for their labor." Ecclesiastes 4:9.

Our first child—a son—came in 1976. We were overjoyed especially because he was born on my husband's birthday. I had a difficult pregnancy and a doubly difficult delivery. At the birth of our son, I received a total of twenty floral arrangements. This had the nurses wondering who I was. Our happiness was short-lived, however, when after a few months our son developed what seemed to be a chest cold and had to be hospitalized. The doctors claimed that he had a growth on his thymus gland.

He was transferred from Port of Spain General Hospital to Caura Hospital, where we spent a whole morning outside the hospital while the surgery was being done. According to the doctors, everything had gone well. The next morning, as soon as we got to the hospital and looked at the nurse's face, we knew something was wrong. Our little boy had died. Apparently the nurse on the morning shift had not been informed that our son had had surgery and had given him a bottle. He choked on it and died. Many people thought that this was cause for a lawsuit, but we were too distraught to pursue it.

We opted, however, to visit my sister in England and take a Cosmos tour to Europe. This helped to ease the pain, only to some extent, because we had to return home to deal with all his clothes, etc. When we looked at the preparation we had made for this child, we decided we would donate all his things to a children's home. Arising out of this, we decided that every year we would make a contribution to a home, and that has continued up to this day.

The Lord will work out his plans for my life—
for your faithful love, O Lord, endures forever.
Don't abandon me, for you made me.
Psalm 138:8

CHAPTER 15
PREPARING TO RESIGN

To resign from a permanent, pensionable job took a lot of planning, strategizing and a lot of prayers, bearing in mind I had to contribute to the household. I was about to leave the known for the unknown.

My first task was to test the market to see how the public would react to the product I was offering. I started by catering for children's parties, doing all the items that children liked: traffic light biscuits, Madeleines, assorted sweets, eclairs, etc. My children's friends in school always looked forward to receiving goodies, which I made for their birthday parties. All this went very well, except that doing this was very time-consuming and the returns were not very attractive. It dawned on me that food was much more profitable. In discussing this with my Chinese friend, he told me that the Chinese man knew this a long time ago, so I decided to concentrate on food only.

One of the requirements for accessing the I.D.C. loan meant that I had to do a feasibility study in my area among the businesses to see whether there was a demand for food outlets or cafeterias such as mine. I gave my business the name *Industrial Caterers* and prepared letters and mailed them to the various industries. The reports coming out of this approach were favorable, but I also was subjected to an interview. A large company, which was a prospective client, sent representatives to my home to enquire about my experience and my capabilities. While this was happening, I was hoping that no one asked to see my facility, because then I was operating out of my little ten-by-ten domestic kitchen. A few days later, I was given the job of catering for 1,000 people for their annual sports day.

My experience up to that time was limited to small home parties and weddings. The compliments I received gave me the feeling that I was up to the task. The job included preparing hamburgers (in those days patties had to be made from scratch), hot dogs, curries, fried chicken, chicken pelau, etc. Families and friends came out to help. We spent the night preparing some of the items for the next day. All went well, but I learnt some valuable lessons in the process. We didn't have proper refrigeration nor proper storage facilities; nor was I aware of some of the basic rules to be followed in bulk food preparation. As a result, we got some unfavorable feedback.

However, the money I got from this job enabled me to erect a new kitchen. I started doing a few weddings and parties on the weekends, thereby gaining invaluable experience. One thing I found out early in the game is that you never agree to share a function with another caterer because you may end up taking blame for someone else's mistakes. Neither do you volunteer information about your recipes.

I remember what happened at an event we were catering for in Chaguanas. Everyone was complimenting us on the sandwiches we had made. While I was willingly giving out recipes, someone whispered to me how silly I was to be so generous. My reply to him was I always obliged but I always omit the main ingredient; in that case it was the roasted peanuts. In this business, I realized one must have a secret ingredient or an unusual item that will always be the talking point. So whatever ideas I had I knew to keep them a secret.

I remember also when I applied for my big loan from the I.D.C., I told very few people, but word spread like wildfire because I was an ex-employee of the corporation. Some people wished me well, while others wondered whether I knew what I was doing. Believe it or not, one loans officer whom I considered a friend, actually hid my application, and refused to submit it. When I called this officer to find out the status of my loan, she informed me that the board was already in session, and that my request had been submitted too late.

After hearing this I felt very depressed because I was in the process of submitting my resignation and would now have to wait a further three months until the board sat again. That little still voice that always spoke to me, which I will explain later, told me to call her secretary, who also was my friend. I argued with that inner voice, saying it was pointless asking someone junior when her boss had already told me it was not possible. I finally decided to call my junior friend, whom I would name Ms. F. I heard Ms. F. in the background telling her boss, "How could you tell Pearl it was too late for the application to go in? It is right on your desk. Furthermore, I will submit it myself." My friend presented my application to the committee while the meeting was in progress. The loan was approved the same day.

It is also important to note that I first approached my bank for a loan to purchase equipment. I always enjoyed a good relationship with my bank when I had to purchase household equipment, cars, etc. However, as soon as I mentioned that I was looking for a loan to start my business, they showed no interest. My friend from the bank, upon hearing that I had approached the I.D.C. for a big loan, called to find out whether I knew what I was doing.

I should mention that before the loan was approved I had to present a letter from the Public Health Department, verifying that my place was suitable for the setting up of a food business. This was the most difficult nut to crack. Nobody knew me, neither did I have an air of importance. I wrote to the Public Health Department asking for assistance; when they failed to respond to my letter, I decided to visit the office myself. I spoke to a Mr. Narine, referring him to the letter I had sent, and again emphasizing that this was a requirement of the I.D.C. when one is applying for a loan.

This gentleman was not interested in visiting the site; his reason was that he couldn't visit a business that was not in existence. Knowing how important it was that I receive that letter, I decided that I wouldn't leave without it. Around 3.30 p.m., when the office was about to close, an elderly man, all dressed up in a suit, noticed that I had been standing outside for the entire day. He motioned me inside and asked whether he could help. After I explained my problem, he called Mr. Narine, dictated a letter to him and handed it to me. It was then I realized that this elderly gentleman was probably Mr. Narine's senior or supervisor. This letter now enabled me to return to the I.D.C. to complete the process for the loan application.

In the meantime, I had several follow up visits to Mr. R. from the School Nutrition company. In one of the visits Mr. R. told me to visit three schools in the area to find out whether they would be willing to accept meals. After speaking to their various boards, two schools accepted meals. Mr. R.'s assistant provided me with a stove, together with some other equipment to commence operation with these two schools.

Everything came together at the same time. I then had to return to the I.D.C. to collect my cheques. That morning, instead of being happy, I came out of the building with the biggest headache. First, I had just been given a contract to feed 300 children and secondly, I had to pay 10% of the value of the vehicle to the Motor Company before receiving the van. At this time, I knew I had reached a dead end because I had absolutely no money. I began thinking that maybe I could use my husband's car to transport the meals. However, finding the money to purchase the foodstuff to supply the meals was quite another story. I stumbled out of the Loan's Officer's office smiling brightly to him and my other colleagues because finally I had gotten through, but they had no idea that I had a big problem to solve.

As I walked along the pavement not seeing or hearing anything, I felt a hand grab my shoulders. When I looked up, it was the Financial Comptroller of a large bank. I knew him because we had worked together at the M.D.C. I exclaimed, "You are the man I want to see!" He said, "What you want, money?" I said "Yes." He said, "Come and see me this afternoon." I didn't hesitate; I got to the bank before him. I spelled out my problem. He then took me into the manager's office.

While sitting there, I was thinking: Here am I in this manager's office, telling him about my business plan, while the bank I was dealing with for years wouldn't even give me a hearing.

After I explained my position to the manager, he listened carefully and said that even though my plan sounded feasible, I had to get a sales forecast done; so, I hustled out of his office and went back to my old office. Remember, my office had a department set up to assist people to start up and manage small businesses. So that part was easy. I went directly to an accountant who started to work immediately on preparing a sales forecast for me. At the end of it, he told me it looked very good and that he didn't foresee a problem.

The following day I was ushered back into the bank manager's office—a potential customer. He looked at my well-prepared proposal and said it looked very promising, but he was foreseeing a problem. He suggested that I didn't need a loan because at the end of each month I would encounter the same problem. In fact, he suggested that I take an overdraft instead, so I could better manage my income and expenditure issues. I was given the overdraft and I was well on the way. Thirty years later, I am still a customer of that bank, with an overdraft far surpassing the initial amount.

Rosina Robinson was the big caterer at that time, and she did all of the catering for participants attending training courses in our office. This is where I met some of her servers. I recruited them to work for me on weekends. However, when I began to cater for the school feeding program, I needed regular workers and I was able to hire two of them because they had the experience I needed.

"And God is able to make all grace abound toward you;
that you, having all sufficiency in all things,
may abound to every good work."
2 Corinthian 9:8

CHAPTER 16
BUSINESS EXPERIENCE

In 1986 we decided to open Avocado Restaurant Ltd. The idea of opening a restaurant came about when it dawned upon me that there was not a single restaurant in the Tunapuna area providing local foods. What I didn't realize at the time was that approval had to be obtained from the Public Health Department before opening a facility to sell food to the public. I got to the point of almost being prosecuted, but I got off with a warning and was told to correct this error right away. Avocado existed for almost three years, serving mainly local foods.

According to some of the businesses in the area, we were able to attract clients from all over because of our marketing strategy. For example, when the Mighty Sparrow, a well-known calypsonian, came to the restaurant with his entourage, it created quite a stir. It was after several visits from customers from the University of the West Indies (UWI) that we were able to get several UWI jobs, including catering for the UWI Credit Union.

A number of people in Tunapuna, who knew of my background and how I arrived from the country to the district a few years earlier, seeking refuge by my brother, were taken by surprise at my achievement. On one occasion, I was reminded of my humble beginnings in the presence of my employees, by a customer who apparently felt that he was entitled to larger portions and loudly expressed his displeasure, using a few choice words. I recalled we both lived on the same street in

Tunapuna. He certainly was not happy at my progress!

I did most of my shopping for myself, sometimes visiting the wholesale market as early as 2.00 a.m. One vendor volunteered to do some shopping for me, claiming he was a farmer. After examining his prices, I realized that his prices were inflated because he did not have his own garden, but made a living by purchasing from farmers. Over the years, I realized that vendors have more marketing skills than university graduates, especially when it relates to the restaurant business.

I stood in the market one day and observed dozens of people purchasing fish from a vendor and couldn't understand why his product was so much cheaper than the vendors in other places. When I observed him closely I realized he was robbing people at the scale. When he was about to do the same to me, his accomplice hinted to him that I was the lady from the restaurant, and he should be careful. Another time, I had asked this same vendor to purchase eighty pounds (80 lbs.) of fish for me, which he delivered and for which he received his payment. I didn't own a large scale, but as soon as he left I went to the nearby grocery and weighed the fish. As I suspected, it weighed less—only sixty-six pounds (66 lbs). That was the last time I had people purchasing for me.

My first attempt at running a retail business taught me a great deal. As soon as I got to the area, all the banks in the area patronized me but in return they all expected me to do business with their bank. I remember one bank gave their workers chits for lunches, and they patronized us each day; however, when they found out that we were dealing with another bank, they withdrew their support. In fact, after visiting this bank and introducing myself to the manager, he attempted to belittle me by addressing me as the assistant manager. I had to let him know that I was the owner/ manager. On another occasion, I saw a different side of how banks operate, when I found a bank manager waiting at the side of my van. She had seen the sign on my van advertising our services and proceeded to introduce herself and to solicit my patronage.

I remember the day also when members of the surrounding business community came to pay me a visit, seeking to find out who was the owner of this restaurant. I won't forget the look on their faces when I introduced myself as the manager. They went on to welcome us in the area and told us what a difference we had made because customers were coming into the area from all parts of Trinidad.

One problem that we had to contend with was stealing. It came in so many forms, some of them so creative I often fell prey to them. For instance, one day a popular radio personality came to me selling promotional packages for his radio station. In an effort to convince me, he produced cheques he had gotten from businesses in the area. In addition, he knew my cashier, so I eventually agreed to buy one of the packages. Days later, I found out that he was no longer employed with the company and was not authorized to collect monies on their behalf.

I also remember one morning at about 4.00 a.m. as I was preparing for the day, I was sitting at the cash register putting in the startup money or "float" for the day. I heard a loud noise on the roof as though someone was running. I looked outside the glass door just in time to see armed policemen with guns pointed towards me. From the nearby police station, they had seen bandits trying to gain entry into the building. The police responded and saw me at the cash register. I raised my hands, trying to indicate my innocence. I felt that morning I could have lost my life. Luckily, I was known to the cops because they all frequented the restaurant. While the police were concentrating on me, however, the bandits made good their escape.

Arising out of the popularity of Avocado Restaurant came an offer to run the Law School Cafeteria. This one was a challenge because I single-handedly had to manage the three places. My husband continued teaching and I did not have a family member or supervisor who could have taken the burden off my shoulders. One thing I have learned the hard way in business is that you don't completely trust people close to you. They look only at the profits and never the hard work that goes into it.

My morning usually started at around 2.00 a.m. I would go to the wholesale market, do my shopping and then deliver to the Law School

Cafeteria, Avocado Restaurant and then to Industrial Caterers. Later on, I would try to return around the busy lunch time period to the two places where cash purchases were being made. One Friday I was at the register in the restaurant and at the end of the day I noticed it was the largest amount of money I had received since opening.

I mentioned this to the cooks, and they told me that that was not the busiest day they had ever seen. In fact, the busiest Friday was on the Fridays when the county council workers got paid. I decided to follow this up, only to realize that monies were being pilfered. I encountered a similar problem at the Law School where monies were also being stolen. I realized that I had to stop the hemorrhage because we were losing money.

The biggest theft occurred at Industrial Caterers when I put one of my family members to handle payments to suppliers. I would sign cheques and leave them with him to make payments. One day, in going through my returned cheques, I noticed considerable amounts being paid to this individual. It was hard to believe that somebody you had trusted and whom you had often given assistance would resort to stealing from you. That day I went to the station and reported him.

I told them I didn't want to charge him, I only wanted to frighten him to see whether he would return the money. The officer was so upset that such a close family member would be so dishonest that he said if given the okay he would put him behind bars. That day, when he found out that the cops were looking for him he returned a small part of the money. The rest he had already invested in a business in Tobago.

All around, I had to deal with dishonest people. There was this cleaner who would come in early to clean the restaurant. One day she was ill and couldn't report for work. It was then we realized that she was selling coffee and tea to passers-by early in the morning. In addition, she would help herself to most of the meats, etc., we had prepared for use later during the day. The cooks realized the items they had prepared the previous day were often short when they turned up for work. I always hated to search people's bags, but a quiet search of handbags led me to see why I was losing money from the various cakes and sweets I had purchased wholesale to make a profit.

Stealing at Industrial Caterers was often cleverly done and involved a lot of creativity. For instance, some staff members would come to work with their Thermos filled with a drink from home and leave with it filled with oil. Some would take home chicken trimmings as pet food but hide chicken parts in between. Sometimes those going out to serve at parties would withhold most of the food meant for the guests and secretly take it home. There was a time when after a big function, one worker was seen clearing the tables and removing the tablecloths, taking them downstairs to the vehicle. When confronted, it was found that he was taking away all the remaining liquor from the party. After hearing reports of what happened at one party, I had to fire eight of my workers for stealing at that party and sullying the company's name.

This is when I decided that because there was hardly anybody I could trust, it was better to close the two outlets and concentrate on one business where I could monitor things more closely.

In operating a small business, your focus is always on making a profit. Getting off the ground and starting to see profits is always top priority. Later on, it dawns on you that a large part of that profit has to be returned to the government in one form or the other. It is a reality you have to face.

In this regard, we have had to pay a lot of interest and penalties to the government which could have been avoided if we had had the right accountant. Our National Insurance (NIS) payments were always up to date, so much so that when it was time for employees to make claims, their contributions were up to date. At one time we were audited by NIS because they didn't realize that most employees worked only during the school term. Our records confirmed the period of work and that workers' contributions had been paid.

Accountant number one, Mr. O'Neal, took advantage of my ignorance for a long time. He collected cheques for making VAT payments and after a period of time, I realized that payments were not being paid.

This resulted in my having to repeat the payments, this time with interest. The same was the case with income tax. We soon realized that this creative accountant would ask us to make cheques payable to him or to some other fictitious company, but he was not paying our taxes to the government. This resulted in my first audit. When the auditor realized that we hadn't filed for a number of years, he decided to help bring us up to date.

The bank kept insisting that I needed a qualified accountant because my records were not being done properly; so, I hired accountant number two. At one stage, interest payments were so high that I had to go into the Chairman, Board of Inland Revenue, to ask for a waiver. The gentleman was very understanding and realized that I was experiencing a problem that a lot of small business people had. One bit of advice he gave was that taxes should be paid quarterly so we would not end up in a similar problem. After searching for an accountant, I was introduced to Mr. Morris. He again was never up to date with payments and again this resulted in my having to make unnecessary interest payments.

Recently we had to tender for a new contract and submit a number of financial statements and annual reports and, thankfully, my accountant had everything up to date. This experience convinced me that at long last I had gotten a reliable, qualified accountant.

We did a lot of functions for the Catholics, such as the Catholic Teachers' Conventions, and various seminars for Catholic teachers. Then there were the Principals' Association functions, TTUTA functions, including Caribbean Union of Teacher's Games, the Girl Guides Association, and several ministries, all arising out of our dealing with the school feeding program.

I remember an incident at the end of one school term. My family and I had just arrived in Texas for a much-needed rest when someone texted me to let me know the Ministry of National Security was trying to contact me. After one phone call I was on the next flight, headed back home. The job in question was very lucrative, catering for a residential program for youths.

Things didn't always go well. There was the time when we were given dates well in advance for a training program. We were catering for a group of four hundred (400), serving morning snacks and lunches. However, there was a mix up in one of the dates, and we were informed at the last minute that snacks and lunches were to be provided on a day that was not on our list. We got that information at about 8:00 a.m. Now bear in mind the morning break was due to start at 10.00 o' clock. I had to give credit to my workers for being able to make that event successful.

My most memorable event was when we were asked to cater for 900 people. We were to provide dinner, dessert, a special menu for children and a wet bar, using proper glassware, cutlery and crockery. The event was being held for retired principals at the Convention Centre. We were asked to arrive at least an hour before starting time, starting time being 7.00 p.m. The first problem we had was that the elevator was out of service, so having to use the staircase with wares, food and drinks presented us with a huge challenge.

The program got underway at about 8.00 p.m. with retirees coming from every corner of Trinidad; some from as far as Matelot, Toco, Icacos, etc. The children came and did their presentation. They arrived early and were given their snack boxes. However, at the end of their performances they were requesting dinners. Seeing that the function had not yet ended, we were asked not to serve. It was hard to deny the children, so we had to purchase food from the nearby KFC out of our own pockets to appease the children.

The program went much longer than was expected and some principals who had to travel long distances asked that at least we would give them dinner to take with them. Some of those retirees who claimed to be diabetics pleaded with us to comply with their request. I made the decision to open one of the food stations (there were five) to facilitate them by at least providing boxed takeaway dinners. The formal program ended around 12.30 a.m. We got a lot of complaints from workers who again had to use the stairs to take the wares back to the vehicles. In this instance, even though those managing the event expressed their displeasure because we had served some people before the function had ended, I had absolutely no remorse because I felt that I had done the right thing.

On another occasion, we were asked to cater for a bank's Christmas dinner. Our instructions were that dinner was to be served at 6.00 p.m. The event was in Chaguanas, and we were located in Trincity. We always take great care to prepare things such as the rice last. I hate to be late for any event, so we arrived at the venue in time to have everything ready for 6.00 p.m. When we arrived there was no one present, not even a representative from the bank. We needed to have certain areas open because there were a lot of insects, and we couldn't open the food. People didn't start arriving until about 9.00 p.m.

The fete—because that's what it turned out to be—didn't start until about 11.00 p.m. and at that time we started worrying about the wholesomeness of some of the dishes, such as the vegetable rice (the holding time for vegetable rice being five (5) hours). People started eating around 12.00 a.m. and when we began serving the rice we knew we had a big problem. The rice and some of the other items had begun to spoil. Around 2.00 a.m. people were still joining the lines for food. In this business the customer is always right, so up to this date, I count this and other incidents as experience. As far as possible, one must seek to get detailed information on the serving times.

"And whosoever shall give to drink
unto one of these little ones
a cup of cold water only in the name of a disciple,
verily I say unto you, he shall in no wise lose his reward."
Matthew 10:42

CHAPTER 17
OVERCOMING TRIALS

My involvement with the School Feeding Program started with serving two schools and later it included several other schools in the east. During that early period, I cooked, I drove and also delivered the meals. Initially, the reception from schools and parents in the area was far from welcoming. Many questions were asked, many assumptions were made because I wasn't known in the area.

School Feeding menus were expected to be followed as given, but I remember the day when one vice principal handed me the menus she thought I should follow, including coo coo with callaloo and steamed fish. Failing to follow her menus, and not adhering to other rules set down by this VP, resulted in her having me reported. An officer from the school feeding program visited the area and consulted with some of the most respected principals. The feedback from them was that they were quite satisfied with the service I was providing.

I was aware that I was in an enviable position being the only caterer in the Tunapuna/ Arouca area, so it was no surprise when, one day, a test of the meals being served to the children in these areas was "found to be contaminated". A strongly worded letter came from management threatening to close our facility. I remember one principal telling me if bacteria were found in my food it should be found in many other homes. I was called into the manager's office, but before going I decided to go on a fast. I couldn't understand how a hot pot of macaroni with chili, together with a lettuce and tomato salad, was found to contain pathogens. So, I went to the office all prayed up.

While waiting to go in to see the manager, I started speaking to a very knowledgeable officer and pointing out to her that if we had taken every precaution in preparing the food and bacteria was found it meant that every other caterer preparing the same menu, who also might not have sanitized the vegetables used, should have run into the same problem. Her advice to me was that I should put this in writing and present it to management. I sat there and penned a letter to the Director.

The following week there was a big headline in the newspapers where employees at a firm in the east had decided to stop work because the same bacteria was found in their water supply. A Public Health Officer later explained that very often in the rainy season, the banks of the Caroni River would flood, contaminating most of the vegetables. It was from this incident sanitizers were introduced into the program, first starting with Condi's Crystal, and later bleach was added as a sanitizer.

Oil prices plummeted to nine dollars per barrel in 1986 and there was immediate closure of the school feeding program. We had also just finished closing down the businesses at the Law School and Avocado Restaurant. This was a difficult period for all of us as we had invested heavily in catering for the school feeding program.

In response to this turn of events, I purchased a mobile food truck and I had it parked on Chacon Street in Port of Spain. We began retailing boxed lunches from it. There was one particular day when one friend from my previous workplace saw me selling from the mobile food truck. She apparently relayed this to others, and they all came out, not to make purchases, but to witness this spectacle. This in no way bothered me because in the past I used to marvel at those Syrian ladies selling food from their trucks while sporting huge diamonds on their fingers, when folks like me with a steady job could hardly afford much.

At the closure of the school feeding program, the government owed us a lot of money and we had a large overdraft to be cleared. We foolishly believed that because the government owned some shares in the

National Commercial Bank, they would forgo some of our interest payments to this bank. This did not happen because at the end of six months when we were eventually paid, we had to pay the overdraft along with all interest charges.

A lot of us caterers began selling off our vehicles and equipment, all at the same time, so it meant that we were selling cheaply. I remember selling a pretty new Suzuki van for very little. The buyer came with cash in a brown bag. Three weeks later, I saw the same van parked on a street with a For Sale sign on it. When I approached the driver, I was surprised to find out that he was asking for much more than I had just sold it for.

A lot of caterers felt that even though we were supposed to re-start the program at a later period, it would be too late to pick up the pieces, so many of them left the country. It is to be noted that the closure of the school feeding program didn't only affect caterers, but resulted in a loss of jobs for many, including fruit suppliers. There were banana suppliers who had supplied us with hundreds of bananas per week. Then there were the citrus suppliers, who most times, supplied already peeled oranges.

I had, of course, to hire fewer workers. In fact, I did all the cooking at that time and had a driver to do the deliveries. Scaling down on the manpower resulted in a grave mishap on one occasion. I had single handedly prepared a sumptuous lunch for a seminar in Port of Spain. While the driver and one helper were climbing the steps, the food container fell from their hands causing a mix up of all the food and creating a huge mess to the company's carpet. Of course, we had to pay for the damage, and that was the end of our dealing with that company.

However, this didn't deter us. We sold all our restaurant equipment to clear our debts, and continued catering for weddings, parties and business seminars. I had hoped to get jobs from friends who worked in different governments agencies but, for a large part, this did not materialize. I got small jobs, like supplying refreshments for afternoon small business programs run by M.D.C. The ex-Mayor of Port of Spain had us do lunches for a number of business programs he was conducting over a six-day period, and a bank manager had us do lunches for some special sessions he was doing for branch managers. This one was very interesting, because the program was being conducted by Marguerite Gordon on Etiquette for Managers. This was quite a challenge because we had to have the table settings just right. This entailed going back to the books and doing a refresher course. In an event like this, I always had resources I could call upon.

The Restructured School Feeding Program

The program re-opened in 1989, this time as the re-structured school feeding program, complete with new management. I remember the then Minister of Education saying to us that this program was not intended to provide jobs for us caterers, but instead to provide meals to the nation's children. Instead of serving meals five days per week, we would now only provide meals three days per week. This new arrangement would last for a while.

By then a number of other things had also changed. Officers visited every day while we were supplying lunches and made regular visits to the schools. On one occasion, a principal had asked that her teachers slice and serve the portions of watermelon to the students. When the officer visited the school and saw what was taking place, she made it known that this practice was unacceptable and was not to recur.

At the end of each term, we had meetings with the principals. This is when principals would express their satisfaction or dissatisfaction with their assigned caterer. There was an instance where a principal brought a sample of the fruit supplied to his school which he found to be unsatisfactory. Such criticism would often cause caterers to panic because their shortcomings could be exposed. On the other hand, these meetings also caused principals to get a greater understanding of what preparing bulk meals entailed, and why certain food items or menus could not be entertained.

When I was asked to cater for a Seventh Day Adventist school that was purely vegetarian, I realized that vegetarian meant much more than extracting the meat from a menu. Also, I learnt in catering for adults that when we used pumpkin loaf and split peas loaf for vegetarians, it was always well accepted. I was able to recommend these items together with mock chicken drumsticks which is still being used on the school feeding menu to this day. One day our nutritionist, Ms. Lodge, asked each caterer to prepare a menu of their choice. My choice was curried channa, pumpkin choka, paratha roti and mango. This menu is still popular up to this day.

Because I had spent most of my life catering to the nutritional needs of children, I felt that I could make a contribution. Sometimes my ideas were accepted, sometimes they were not. While visiting the US, I sometimes would have breakfast at a Target store where they would sell breakfast pizzas. I found this interesting and suggested that this could be added to our breakfast menu. Another menu that I saw some time ago was sautéed spaghetti with rich tomato sauce and chicken franks with onions at the top. I served this menu to a school one day and the children danced.

In our attempt to serve fresh fruits, we would sometimes travel to Toco and other places to purchase an entire fruit tree. We tried the same thing with mangoes, but the schools complained that the mangoes created a problem in the school yards. We tried using grapes, which the children loved. However, management preferred the use of local fruits. In addition, after a while, grapes proved to be too expensive.

Over the years we have made several structural and other changes to our facility in accordance with advice from management of the School Feeding Program. Profits from school feeding are usually small, but we have been able to survive because of the quantity of meals supplied per day. With the profits came the expenditure for the upgrades because we were often asked to make changes aimed at improving the facility. Since starting the business, we moved from wooden to laminated counter tops and tables, to stainless steel surfaces; we have installed convection ovens, and have changed from plastic containers to insulated totes. At one point, we were convinced that most of the profits were going back into making improvements.

Most of us caterers changed from being sole traders to registered companies. One manager advised that this should be done for the purpose of continuity. Putting our business in this category involved increased taxes and a lot of other red tape. At the start, many of us couldn't see the value this would bring to our business. In fact, many of the changes, when implemented, met with opposition from many of the caterers.

The biggest change came with the introduction of Hazard Analysis Critical Control Points (HACCP). Caterers had to undergo special training to understand the concept and to put the points into practice. In addition, renovation had to be undertaken to rearrange areas to ensure proper receiving, storage and preparation were in place, in accordance with universal standards of sanitation. With HACCP, some of the old methods of cooking, that we had grown accustomed to, had to be changed.

All the training in food preparation over the years was certainly of benefit to me. Thankfully, whether we were catering to children or adults, we have had no casualties because of contaminated food. My thinking as a caterer is always to put people before profits. As a school feeding caterer, having to purchase in large quantities, I am always in a position to offer better prices than the average caterer.

I recall that when the Director at the time, Mr. Denrit, had a grand reception to honor caterers who had contributed to the program for over ten years, and he had somehow omitted my name, I couldn't help but express my disappointment. I said to myself he probably doesn't know my name, but when God knows your name, that is all that matters. My role as a school feeding caterer is, and has always been, to provide wholesome, nutritious meals to the nation's children in a manner that is pleasing to God.

"For with God, nothing is impossible."
Luke 1:37

CHAPTER 18
SETTLING DOWN

There was a time when we conducted the business of school feeding from our tiny three-bedroom house. We allotted half of the house as living accommodation and the other half for food preparation. Bathroom facilities were limited. One bathroom was for staff usage and the other was for our use. There was this time when we had guests visiting from abroad and we had to give them our master bedroom along with our bathroom facilities. To avoid having to use the staff bathroom, very often we had to resort to using the bathroom in the mall. This was the extent of our inconvenience.

After hearing complaints from the school feeding management about the size of the facility, we decided to give the entire house to food preparation and seek alternative accommodation. We purchased some land very close to the facility with the hope of building. We always had our eyes on lands in that area as the ideal place for building our dream house. So, our initial plan was to rent a property, hoping to complete our building within a short space of time. We had in mind a particular architect/contractor because we always liked his work. I have found it amazing how people can draw up their plans and get their project completed in record time, but this was not so in our case.

In fact, from our experience, we have found that we always have to fight to get what we wanted. After months of meetings and adjustments to the plans, the project was eventually started. Everything went wrong: the contractor failed to comply with our request in many cases, monies placed in his hands were not accounted for, and on and on it went. The problems were so many that we decided to sell the property together with the building material already purchased. We felt that this was not God's plan for us because suddenly we lost interest in owning a property in that area.

Soon after this fiasco, the house we were renting in Montague was sold and we had to obtain another rental property in a hurry. In going through the newspapers, we came across an ad for the rental of a house in the Valsayn area, so we decided to move there. I remember saying to my husband that I didn't particularly like Valsayn, but I believe the Lord had us going to this area for a reason. When we got to the area, we were dismayed when we saw the dilapidated state of the house; however, just as we were hesitating, another prospective renter came along, and we showed immediate interest again.

Because we needed to move urgently, we decided to take this house which apparently had not been occupied for a long time. There were bats in the ceiling, flying frogs in the bathroom, large trees with all sorts of animals on them, and rusting pipes. And to crown it all, the next-door neighbor had a mini zoo, so that sometimes we would wake up to find monkeys on the cars. We weren't particularly welcomed in the area, and not even some friends whom we had known for years would throw us a lifeline. Because of the rusted pipes, most times we had to get water from the kitchen in Trinity and also do our cooking there.

We indicated to our realtor that we weren't interested in the Valsayn area, but she insisted on showing us some properties. There was a property that we liked, but our old attitude led us to believe that we couldn't afford it. This house was owned by a family of pilots. They were very particular as to whom they wanted to sell the house. However, they decided to consider us because they liked our children. After we had prayed about it and spoken to our bankers, they decided after looking at our figures that we were in a position to make the purchase. Because of our ages though, we were given four years to complete the payment.

This meant that our mortgage was extremely high--an almost impossible situation--so I promised the Lord that if I was able to clear this mortgage within the allotted time, I would have the biggest thanksgiving service. We ventured into the purchase of this house by faith. With our old civil service mentality, we couldn't conceive the idea of paying for a house in four years.

The four years came by very quickly and we did have the biggest thanksgiving service, complete with church band and singers. Of course, after the message delivered by my Pastor, I gave the feature address, sharing this story, and other testimonies.

"Let the redeemed of the Lord say so,
Whom He has redeemed from the hand of the adversary"
Psalm 107:2

CHAPTER 19
TESTIMONIES

God Heals

I remember one day standing downstairs of my mother's house and leaning on the little Austin motor car her husband had. It was one of my very bad days, when I was faced with hopelessness. I stood there in my little black and white dress that my sister had purchased in a jumble sale and asked God, if he was alive to reveal himself to me. He did in a most unexpected way.

Even though I had always attended Church schools, religion and the fear of God meant nothing to me except to make fun of people who professed to serve God. In secondary school, for instance, there was this boy and his brother who were very poor. Rumour had it that their church was supporting them. Rusty was the older brother's name. He had a lot of bad teeth and in fact he was so aesthetically challenged that we nicknamed him Handsome. He was always handing out religious tracts and having lunchtime prayer meetings.

One day, Rusty invited us to a crusade hosted by a visiting evangelist. I went with a group of my friends just to sing and clap and make fun of everybody and everything. Of course, Rusty was walking around handing out his tracts and ministering. At this time in my life, I used to suffer with a very bad head cold. I didn't know the correct name of this condition, but my parents called it "catta", for I had this head cold which came with discolored mucous and an offensive smell. (Now I know it is called catarrh.)

Coming to the end of the service, the minister asked people to place their hands on the part of their bodies where they had an ailment. I looked down and placed my hand on my head very inconspicuously while he prayed. As soon as he was finished I took a deep breath and the smell I had before was gone! I did that a few times and was no longer smelling anything offensive. That head cold and that funny smell never returned. Years later, I had occasion to visit a government ministry, and to my surprise, there was Mr. Rusty seated at his own desk, dressed in a long-sleeved, crisp white shirt, with straightened teeth, looking like a professional. I thank God for using Rusty to get me to the place where I could receive my healing.

Now when I look back on my life I realize that over and over again God has revealed himself to me in a number of ways. All the suffering, all the pains, all the sicknesses only served to make me strong, so now that I am older, whenever I face a crisis, I know how to get on my knees and cry out to God. People often ask why I don't often go up to the altar for prayers. My answer is always: "I spoke to him this morning. He knows, He sees, He hears, and He always responds." I have found that in life, every step of the ladder you climb, someone is waiting to pull you down. So, I have learnt through my many experiences how to put on the full armor of righteousness and to stand, trusting in God who is my Healer, and so much more.

Saved and Set Free

Once upon a time in my life I never believed that there was a real enemy waiting to kill, steal, destroy and create havoc in one's life. I would hear stories from other people and listen to incidents of spiritual attacks they were experiencing but always dismissed them as fiction. In fact, my mother claimed to have special powers which she said she had gotten from a Venezuelan spiritualist. She claimed it was a gift of healing.

Very often I would observe persons visiting my mother in search of healing and to get answers to other spiritual problems. Also, every year there would be occasions where Ma would prepare large amounts of food as a form of thanksgiving. It always bothered me as a child that nowhere in the midst of giving thanks were there any signs of prayer being said, not even the recital of the Lord's Prayer.

My mother once explained to me that this special gift of healing would be handed over to me. She tried over and over to explain the workings of this gift that she was about to transfer to me, but I paid little attention because as I said, I didn't see any prayer in her practices. My unwillingness to accept her offer, or to show any willingness to at least understand, is what resulted in my getting spiritually ill for a long time. My sickness, which included sleepless nights, strange visitations, etc., took a toll on me.

After my mother passed, this led me to a lot of places seeking someone who would understand and relieve me of this burden. I was finally introduced to Pastor Duncan's church in Curepe, where he had his large, lunch time healing services. At this church I got my first real understanding of the kind of spiritual problems that existed in this world. I couldn't sleep for days after I witnessed the deliverance of a bright, pretty little girl who had just passed the Common Entrance Exam for a prestige school. As Pastor prayed, she would scream and the voice coming out of her was the voice of an adult. Pastor enquired from her who had sent the attack and she called names. As he ministered to her, I witnessed this little girl being completely healed.

Pastor Duncan became so popular and so powerful that he even received a visit from the then Prime Minister, Dr. Eric Williams. It was under Pastor Duncan's ministry, that I accepted the Lord and received such a strong and powerful anointing that every other force had to give way to the power of the Holy Spirit. Later on, I moved on from the Curepe Pentecostal Church and went to another full gospel church. My tithe to this church was so large that my accountant very often used to question the amount. When later on I discovered that, because of poor accounting practices, a large amount of money was stolen, I decided to stop attending church.

For approximately two years I stood at the crossroads, not aligning myself to any church. I was so disenchanted. One day, a friend invited me to my current place of worship, citing the pastor as truly a man of God. I sat in that church Sunday after Sunday, placing him and his ministry under scrutiny, before deciding whether this was a good place to make my home church and to tithe. After 32 years, I am serving the Lord and receiving spiritual food at this same ministry.

At one time, I used to suffer with headaches, but it was not just headaches; it was something of a burning sensation in my scalp. Sometimes it felt like pins and needles and other times like a ball of fire. I would apply all sorts of home remedies, but nothing worked. Telling folks about this complaint proved futile, since nobody seemed to understand.

One day, my friend, David, invited me to Pastor Ramsahai's church in Port of Spain. Normally, whenever I visit a church for the first time, I always behave like a cow and smell the grass before eating it. At the end of the message, the Pastor proceeded to call out different ailments, as the Spirit led him. People were forming lines to receive prayer from the Pastor. As I listened, I heard the Pastor describing my ailment and he invited the person with that complaint to come forward. I am never one to always go running to the Pastor for prayer, let alone a strange pastor.

After he repeated the call several times, I eventually joined the line. When I was three persons away from him, he stopped and held on to his head and said, "I am feeling fire! The person with the fire on their head is just inches away from me." When I got to this man of God, he laid his hand on me and said, "My God, how long have you been suffering with this? Today, the God you serve will give you a release."

That church required you to place your offering in the Pastor's hand. When I gave him my offering, which was $100, I remember him saying, "God will not only heal you, but he will cause you to prosper. The enemy will try, but he will not succeed."

God Provides

When I got married, I was a non-church-going Christian, but my husband was a church-going, Bible-believing Christian. It was only after a series of illnesses that I eventually seriously began to seek refuge in the church, and in God. Over and over, God showed me that He was alive and present in my life. The Psalmist says in Psalm 91:11-12, "He will give his angels charge over you to keep you in all your ways, and in their hands they will bear you up lest you dash your foot against a stone."

When we had our first child, we had our monies saved for medical expenses, the nursing home, etc. We never expected that I would have to get surgery, thus putting a demand on our already strained financial resources. So, I went ahead and had the surgery, following which we had little money to take us through to the next salary. We were down to our last $100. I went to church that Sunday, but before putting the money into the collection basket, I lifted it up and reminded God that it was our last $100, and we needed it to see us through. That morning, I prayed and asked God to multiply it. I don't think in my life that I would ever be telling God to stop supplying my financial needs, because what happened after that prayer was amazing.

The next week, first, my father-in-law gave us a huge donation for the baby, then we both received income tax returns. In all, money came from four different sources. We were trying to purchase a play pen in order to leave the baby by my mother-in-law while I was at work. What seemed almost impossible before, we were able to obtain, and so much more. That set me thinking: Indeed, I was serving an Ephesians 3:20 God: "Now unto him that is able to do exceedingly, abundantly above all that we can ask or think."

A similar thing happened to me years ago after I had just gotten a new job. One evening, I had enough in my handbag to travel home but I had no money to travel to work the next day. I was just walking up the street wondering whom I could approach for a small loan to get to work the next day, when I looked across the street and there was a wad of single dollars. When I took it up and counted it, not only was there enough to help with transportation for the next day, but enough for the entire week.

Lost and Found

My sister had died in England, and this was a terrible time for all of us. She had left behind a son who was in his twenties and was able to look after himself, but her only daughter was only eleven and we were concerned about having to leave her in the care of her father alone in England. My brother-in-law thought it best to visit Trinidad to relax and visit the beaches. When they came, we decided to visit a friend's guest house in Blanchisseuse to spend the weekend. I decided to carry along enough money to pay a gas station for our monthly gas bill which I decided to deal with on the return trip. My brother-in-law had also given me his wallet to keep, and that had pounds sterling in it; all of which I had safely tucked away in my handbag.

We had a lovely dinner in Blanchisseuse, and enjoyed a great time just chit-chatting, but we weren't too happy with the accommodation, so we decided to head back home. On our way, we stopped at Las Cuevas beach and a had a swim. We went down to Maracas Bay, purchased some bake and shark and returned home.

When we got home, I realized to my horror that I didn't have my pink handbag with all the cash amounting to quite a tidy sum. We checked in and out of the car, but the handbag was nowhere to be found. At this time, I couldn't face my husband nor my brother-in-law, because they were saying they could not understand how this could have happened. At this point in my life, I had developed such a sweet relationship with my God that I listened to that still soft voice of the Holy Spirit that kept telling me to call the owner of the guest house in Blanchisseuse.

However, I kept saying I saw no reason to call when I knew that when I had left Blanchisseuse I had the hand bag with me. Bear in mind my handbag had my brother-in-law's ID card and other documents in it.

I sensed the Lord would have me lock myself in the room, read Psalm 16, and call on him. I finally decided to listen to the voice of the Holy Spirit and call Mr. Hernandez in Blanchisseuse. I explained to him that I knew it was pointless calling him because I knew I had left with the bag, but decided I would call anyway.

To my surprise, Mr. Hernandez said some of the sweetest words I could ever hear, "Are you speaking about a pink handbag?"

"Yes! Yes!" was my reply.

Mr. Hernandez said, "Hold on; I will call you back." When he did, he said to me, "Mrs. Spring, your handbag is safe." This was the story I got from him: His cousin, who runs the cafeteria on the beach, had the handbag; she had found a lot of money in it but was unable to find a Trinidad address. Mr. Hernandez advised me to go up to Maracas with proper I.D. to receive my handbag from his cousin.

I went to Las Cuevas beach the next day, introduced myself to the cafeteria owner, and this was her reply: "Miss, I don't know who you are, but you have to be a praying woman. I just came off a fast and was standing at the entrance of the cafeteria. The cafe was full, and my husband was calling me to come and help, but I was ignoring him. Just then I saw this car driving off and a pink handbag fell to the ground. I saw the biggest crook on the beach reach for it. I shouted to him, and I told him to bring it to me. When I opened the bag, I noticed that it had a lot of money, but I couldn't find a Trinidad address. Just as I was wondering what to do with the bag, my cousin from Las Cuevas called me."

My offer to pay the lady for her kindness was stoutly refused.

That Still Soft Voice

Throughout my Christian life I have always listened to that gentle, soft voice of the Holy Spirit speaking to me. One Friday at the end of the month, I had gone to the bank to collect salaries. I had reached the stage where I was no longer driving the old Mazda panel van but for the first time had bought myself a new bronze-colored Ford Escape truck.

There weren't many such vehicles around at the time, so it looked pretty conspicuous. I parked on the side street and went into the bank.

As it was the end of the month, the lines in the bank were rather long. I was standing in the queue for close to an hour anxiously awaiting my turn when that voice told me to get out of the line. As usual I started to argue because I couldn't understand why I should leave the line when there were just about two or three persons ahead of me. After this voice wouldn't leave me alone, I decided to leave the bank. I went back to my car and as I was opening the door, this guy who was sitting at the side of the car approached me and demanded that I hand over all the money I had. Thankfully, I had only a few single dollars. (Remember, I had gone to collect salaries). All I remember is that he was brown-skinned, with grey eyes and a foreign accent. I drove off trembling, and thanking God for always giving his angels charge over me.

Another example of hearing that still, soft voice occurred a few years ago when I was running a prestigious cafeteria. Whenever we were closed for a long weekend, we would often visit on the Sunday evening to make sure everything was okay for the start of the work week. On this particular Sunday evening, it was raining heavily and there was thunder and lightning. I had already made up my mind that I was not venturing out in this type of weather. Again, that still, soft voice kept insisting that I should go and check the premises. When I was about to go to bed that voice became so persistent that I decided to defy it and cover my ears with my pillow. The next morning, I decided to rise early and check to see whether all was well. Apparently there had been a plumbing problem the evening before, and the entire cafeteria was flooded. Failing to listen to the Holy Spirit caused me a lot of time and money.

Another time, I was about to travel to New York for the first time to purchase equipment for the restaurant. One friend arranged for me to stay with her family. Another acquaintance, who was in the restaurant business and had a lot of connections, gave me all the information on her New York connections, one such person was named Rob, and said I shouldn't do any purchasing until I had contacted him. When I got to the home of my friend's family, I decided to contact Rob. After making numerous phone calls and not getting a reply from him, I decided that at least I should scout around and just look at the prices. After a while, I told my friend the fact that I wasn't getting a hold of Rob meant that I wasn't supposed to meet him; so, I went ahead and made a substantial number of purchases and made contacts on my own.

I finally got a hold of Rob and told him what I had in mind. He put together his price list and came over to discuss them with me. Many of the items Rob was quoting prices for, I had already bought; and to my utter surprise, they had cost me 10 times less. I knew once again the Lord had protected me. I had spent one week with my friend's cousin, named Yvonne, and when she saw how the Lord was working in my life, she longed for me to remain another week.

Feeding the Needy

One day after leaving service at the church I attended at the time, which was Woodbrook Pentecostal Church, I was passing around Woodford Square and noticed a lot of homeless persons. My first thought was: How are these people receiving meals? On further investigation, I realized that there were a number of people who had no way of receiving meals, including some who had just left their church services. There was one such old lady who stayed at one of the hostels, where after residents left on mornings, they weren't allowed to re-enter until 4.00 p.m., so she had to remain outside until that time. I felt led to do something to help them.

I started providing meals to the homeless and needy who would be in Woodford Square, Tamarind Square, and the two locations of the St Vincent de Paul homes, a home for battered women and several other homes. Everyone in Woodford Square knew my vehicles, so much so that when I would go without the children they would ask for them. One Sunday there was a function at the Town Hall for which we were catering. All the vagrants left the square and gathered around my vehicle.

The authorities could not understand why. I knew, however, that they all knew my vehicle and thought the meals were for them. A lot of people never understood why I reached out to underprivileged children and why I would go back to the country to offer help to families. In fact, some of the same people I helped often described me as stupid.

There was this young girl whom I had seen growing up in one of these homes. She reached the stage where she was about to get married. I was happy for her and decided to provide the wedding cake, the refreshments, etc., to help make her day. This is just one of the many occasions where God gave me the opportunity to help someone in need. I count it a privilege to be able to do this. To Him be all the glory.

Primary School Search

Like most parents, I wanted the best education for my children. When they were little, I had them enrolled in what I considered the best private school. After a few years, we realized that the school the girls were attending was somewhat of a finishing school, complete with ballet, music, and language skills, but they didn't have what it took to get them into the best secondary schools. My husband, being the school teacher he was, gave me an ultimatum: It was either I found a school, or he would find one himself. In fact, he gave me one week to find a school.

My preference was a Catholic private school in the east, but we were too late because you had to register the children at birth, so it was way too late to register them there. One of my children's friends, whose name was Jacinta, was a pupil of this particular school. One night, I had a dream that Jacinta was playing in the schoolyard. This dream baffled me for a while, but I decided to disregard it. A couple of days went by, and I decided to check another school, also in the east, seeking admission for the children.

Someone met me outside the locked gate to let me know it was pointless checking because their registry was booked for a number of years. Just as I was driving away feeling dejected, the Holy Spirit (with that small voice) told me that this was not where he had sent me. He had sent me to the other Catholic school. I began to argue with God and explain to him that I was not a Catholic and I didn't know anyone in that school.

I headed over there in my big old Suzuki van, and decided to drive into the school yard. I learned later that you had to pass through the secretary before going in to see the nun, who was the principal. I came out of the van, went past the security and asked a student where to find the principal's office. This child directed me to the back entrance where only the nuns entered. The principal was surprised to see me but allowed me to enter, nevertheless. That morning, I received such favor from God that the principal spoke to me as a long-lost friend. After sharing with me about all her school's accomplishments, she still went on to let me know that she had no room.

When she saw my surname, she admitted that she had never had anyone with such a surname in her school. She also confessed that the Lord showed her in a dream that she was only giving $100 notes to a certain group of children and $1.00 bills to a lesser group. As we spoke, I gathered she had taken an instant liking to me because she asked me to return the next day with the child's exercise books.

The next day I returned with my daughter's books. Incidentally, my daughter had written an essay about her grandmother, which the nun liked. Sister then decided to call her third grade teacher to see whether there was a vacancy. The teacher indicated there was a vacancy because Jacinta, my daughter's friend, had just been expelled for indiscipline. Indeed, the prayer of the righteous availeth much! Thus began a long relationship with that school, after both my children were admitted.

Our Dream Home

The home we had purchased in Valsayn was old, but it was beyond our wildest imagination. It had two porches, five bedrooms, three bathrooms, one large living room, an equally large dining room, a servant's quarters and a large kitchen. There was also adequate land space with lots of fruit trees. We felt that at long last we had gotten our dream home.

After about five years of living and enjoying this property, we decided that we wanted to do some minor changes to really reflect our wishes. We had our drawings done up and when it was almost time for submission, the draughtman got sick and wasn't able to give us much help. A friend, who always tries to help, recommended a contractor he knew who was from another country. This contractor brought over his workers and had them live on the premises. We had observed a similar situation at a house in another area and we were pleased with their work. The arrangement was that we would move out of the house altogether and the house would be completed in nine months.

We had nine months of problems, instead. In fact, nine months turned into three years. Most of the workers he hired were unskilled, which resulted in a lot of shoddy work being done. At one point, we had to hire a Clerk of Works to examine some of the 'finished work'. We went from making minor adjustments to demolishing the entire house. Even though we had done renovations to our previous house, this one proved too much for us. The resident workers vandalized the property; even destroying the fruit trees in the process.

When we had gone past the scheduled finishing date and the house still had a myriad of problems with no end in sight, we decided to fire the contractor. It didn't end there because we also had to fire the roof contractor because we were having issues with his work. One morning when we felt that we were over our heads because money was running out, the house was in shambles, and we were just clueless, I stood looking outside a half-finished window and wondering, "Lord, what next?"

That same still voice whispered to me to pray and anoint the house. In fact, I was reminded that I had anointing oil in the car. That morning I reclaimed my house from the hands of the enemy. I used the power given by the Holy Spirit 'to bind and combine, to trample and dismantle' and I went from room to room taking back what God had given to me. As a result, we felt a sense of relief, and realized that we were back in the game.

This is when we met Brian, an experienced architect. He decided to re-do the layout. We got a small contractor from Trinidad this time. He spent a great deal of time correcting shoddy work. At that time, we had gone way past our budget. My bank manager decided, however, that she would work with me. At one point we were so over our heads in debt that we thought there was no end in sight; but every time we thought we couldn't finish the roof, a catering job came in. The same was the case with the fence and the ceiling. Brian travelled with us to purchase most of our tiles, bathroom fittings, etc. I realized when dealing with my God that he never ever gives us just the barest minimum--Beans and Rice--it is always more than enough: Ephesians 3:20 blessings!

When the time had come for painting, we contacted a salesman from a paint company. I don't think he knew how helpful he was being when he recommended Miss Charmaine, who turned out to be more than a paint consultant. When she came in and looked around, she said that there was a lot of fine tuning to be done before we could even consider painting. When she told me her price, I couldn't understand what she was talking about because all we wanted was someone who would help with the colors. Charmaine did a fantastic job with the interior, right down to the draperies; so much so, that people were stopping to enquire about who our paint consultant was. In the end, I had to admit that her work was worth much more than she was asking for. Charmaine turned out to be a believer, a professional and an asset to the kingdom.

When everything was completed we realized that what we had envisioned was a far cry from the eventual finished product. The lesson we learnt was that when God has a plan for you don't expect it to go through without setbacks. The enemy will constantly put stumbling blocks in your way to frustrate you because he knows what the finished product will be. I say to folks: Whenever you are facing opposition, bear in mind you are in the right position. Stay the course.

Something else, my husband and I have learnt the hard way: when you are about to receive a blessing from God - get a promotion, buy a new car, do some addition to your house, expand your business - it's best to keep it a secret until it is completed. Bad eyes and bad energies can stymie your progress.

Industrial Relations Problems

As I had been an employee for approximately fifteen years and had worked in the Management Development Centre for a long period I thought I had enough knowledge as to how an employer should relate to workers, but I soon realized that I was dealing with a completely different level of employee and that it required a special understanding of workers' rights.

My first encounter with the Ministry of Labour was when I hired a worker who had often worked with me as a server. We hired her to assist in the kitchen. At the start I realized that she was a bit slow and had a problem getting vegetables to the cooks in a timely manner. She was very emotional and always had problems relating to the other workers.

There came a day when the chef spoke harshly to her and instead of reporting this to the supervisor, she went to the police station and made a report. The station's superintendent informed me that these two workers were to stay at least 20 feet apart from each other. My chef had already worked 30 years with the company and was an excellent worker, whereas this other worker had just joined the company a year before. Of course, I decided to fire the junior person because I felt it was impossible to give this junior person a warning letter if they were not to be in close proximity in the workplace; so, her termination had to be immediate.

This junior employee, whom I will call Sharlene, took the matter to her trade union. Over the years, I have always had satisfied workers. My chef had been in my employ for over 30 years, as I said; my sous chef

24 years, and all others ranged from 10 years and over. So going before a trade union was new to me. After listening to both our cases the union found that she was wrongfully dismissed and insisted that I pay damages amounting to $19,000.

All other workers who knew she was in the wrong sympathized with me, except one handyman. This gentleman, who was a delinquent worker himself, when he learnt that his co-worker was awarded damages, decided that he would now work at his own pace, forcing management to fire him. He was given a warning letter, which he refused to accept, instead challenging management to fire him.

Luckily for us, one day he walked off the job, hoping that we would ask him to return because he knew it was difficult to get a replacement. His plan didn't work because when he returned hoping to be reinstated, we had already gotten a replacement. Mr. Deon had automatically fired himself.

Airport Favor: Heathrow

On our first trip to the United Kingdom, we behaved like little kids; we bought everything that looked different to us. Friends kept warning us against over-buying because the fees on the overweight at the airport were very high. Of course, we couldn't understand this, so we continued our shopping.

The airport was quite a long distance away from where my sister lived in Ilford. We always knew that we should avoid taking the black taxi cab so we called a local taxi driven by a Pakistani man who spoke little English. At the start of our long journey to the airport, I noticed a worried look on my husband's face as he rummaged in his hand luggage. Even though he didn't say much, I knew something was wrong. When we got to the airport my husband couldn't wait for the opportunity to go through the suitcases. This is when I found out that he had forgotten our passports at home. This was about 8.00 a.m. and the flight to Trinidad was due to depart at 10.00 a.m.

Leaving my husband with the suitcases, I decided to take the train back, of course, with the hope that I would get back in time. While on the way, my husband called to let me know that the suitcases had already been weighed and the charges had amounted to 300 pounds sterling. We certainly didn't have an answer to this one. As I travelled back on the train to Heathrow, this time with passports in hand, I started to pray that God would send the answer.

The answer came when I got back to the airport and found out that the flight had been delayed to 4.00 p.m. This was one time when a delayed flight worked to our benefit. That delay took care of part one of our problem; now we had to deal with the 300 pounds overweight charges which we certainly didn't have. On approaching the counter, I looked at the faces of all the counter clerks and selected the one I wanted to check us in.

Knees trembling, we approached this tall, handsome Englishman, still quietly calling on God to intervene. As soon as he saw my name--Douglas-Spring--he wanted to know more about it. Of course, I obliged explaining that my maiden name was Douglas and that I had married a Spring and it was customary in my country to combine both names, making it "double barrelled". As we both laughed at this, knowingly or unknowingly, he allowed all the suitcases to go through without adding the charges and we were on our way home. On the flight back to Trinidad, I couldn't help but praise and thank God for answering my prayers and making a way for me where there seemed to be no way.

Airport Favor: Crown Point

On one occasion, we had gone to Tobago for a weekend with the children. We had a great time moving around and enjoying the island. While bathing at the hotel's swimming pool one day, we observed this family with two little boys. My first thought was that they were foreigners, but our children pointed out that they attended the same school. When the weekend was over, and we got to the airport we realized that we were going to have a problem getting a flight back to Trinidad.

I overheard the parents of these two boys talking about their connections on the board of the airline. I told myself that these people had good contacts and would surely get on the plane before any of us. Just then, we decided to move away from the crowd and sit on some nearby chairs. Miraculously, an attendant came and told us that there were four seats available on a flight and our suitcases would arrive later. We couldn't believe our ears, but we knew it was the favor of God. This made me realize once again that whenever you feel less than, God always let you know that you are more than special in his sight.

Hurricane Harvey

In 2018, I visited my daughter in Houston. She lives in a lovely, gated-community in Cypress. Soon after arriving, I took a stroll at the back of her house, just admiring the lake area with its jogging track, complete with exercise equipment along the pathway. The huge houses, along with the beautiful landscape, all captivated my imagination.

Two days later, we began hearing about a hurricane about to hit the Texas area. However, we decided to still visit my other daughter who lived in Austin to see whether everything was alright with her. Austin was experiencing a lot of high winds and rain so we decided to pack up and head back to Houston so we would all be together. To get an update, we turned on the television, and soon realized that the hurricane was about to hit Houston. Wasting no time, we were on the road back to Houston in pouring rain, with dark clouds hovering over us. Pretty soon it dawned on us that families were packed in cars, trucks and vans heading *out* of Houston and here we were heading *to* Houston. My husband and one of my daughters weren't too happy with the decision to go back to Houston and leave Austin where they felt we would have been relatively comfortable and safe.

In times like these, my only option is to call on God. I said to them, "You all, let's have church." People perhaps thought we were mad because we sang, we clapped, we prayed in tongues, all the while facing dark clouds as we drove towards the hurricane. There was one good thing: we didn't have to face groceries that were already running out of food because we had already shopped in Austin. Incessant rain and heavy winds greeted us. I didn't know very much about hurricanes, because preparing for hurricanes in Trinidad is never taken seriously. We always feel our mountains would protect us and that *God is a Trini*!

When we arrived in Houston, I prepared a Trini comfort dish of curried chicken with potatoes and dhalpouri rotis. Meanwhile the others were taking all the necessary precautions around the house in readiness for this hurricane. We did not have to wait very long before heavy winds began uprooting the trees, and darkness engulfed the area. The heavy rains persisted, overflowing the guttering and resulting in pools of water around the house.

The news coming out of CNN and other networks painted a grim picture, so much so that when my grandson asked us to explain what was being said we would try to sugar coat it. At one time, he had to correct us, telling us we were giving him inaccurate information.

Come nightfall, the lightning, thunder and cracking winds were so loud and frightening that we had to turn the volume up on the television so as to drown out the noises. My family said that they wanted to experience what a real hurricane was like, so they were not going to sleep. Me, I needed my sleep so I said my prayers, recited Psalm 4 with special emphasis on vs. 8, which says, "I will both lay me down in peace, and sleep, for thou Lord maketh me dwell in safety." Sometime in the middle of the night I heard that we had escaped the storm, but the problem we now had to face was the problem of flooding. I went back to sleep, thinking that the worst was over and that we had been spared.

At about 5.00 a.m., my daughter came into my room waking me up and shouting that we were surrounded by water. This was indeed a sight to behold. The same surroundings I had been admiring a few days ago had turned into a sea overnight. The water from the lake had overflowed its banks and was slowly inching its way into the yard. Even though the house was on a slight incline the water was making its way up to the house.

I have experienced floods in Trinidad but that was nothing compared to what I was witnessing. There was no point trying to escape because almost the whole town was under water. I always say that whenever you are faced with a situation like this, you had better know your God and know how to call on Him. I remember running to my room and running back out, looking at the catastrophic. My daughter and her husband were taking furniture upstairs to higher ground.

As I surveyed the scene, I remembered the incident in the Bible where the disciples were on the boat and a storm was raging while Jesus slept. His words to calm the storm were, "Peace, be still!" That morning I called on my God. I know I sounded crazy, but as Christians we all have a little crazy in us. I looked in all directions and shouted, "Peace be still." I rebuked the wind and the rain and prayed that God would roll back this 'Jordan River'.

My son-in-law, who is a seasoned 'hurricane tracker', kept measuring the depth of the water. This I will never forget, because when he checked at the end of the day the water had started to recede. At this time, in areas not too far from us, people were being rescued from rooftops; families and their dogs were seen swimming to safety. A pastor and his wife drowned trying to escape, while a family of six drowned because they didn't know the difference between the lake and the road. We thanked God for answering our prayers that day, because not only did we not suffer any damage, but we were able to provide shelter for other families. Our God is truly awesome! Praise Him!

Cecil's 70th

My husband was about to celebrate his 70th birthday and we wanted to give him something special. In trying to decide on a theme for this grand occasion, the children suggested a cowboy theme, someone else suggested a Hawaiian theme, but none of these suited my husband. However, I remembered that on one of our visits to Europe, Cecil and I were having dinner with a Jewish family, and he was all decked off in his Dashiki and me in a matching African outfit. Some folks thought that Trinidad was some part of Africa and that we were royalties. My husband ordered drinks and laughed loudly, living up to his status of being free-spirited, and his new status of being royalty.

Remembering this, I decided to have the party with an African Safari theme, and make him truly an African Chief for the evening. So, we set about preparing an outdoor space at the southern side of the house, recruiting a church band complete with drummers, and ordering special outdoor safari decorations. Invitations were sent in the mail and every other detail was carefully worked out. However, there was one thing we completely forgot: his function was carded for the beginning of October when there is usually a lot of rain. We were thinking that perhaps when the time came around, we would get a reprieve from the rain.

We went ahead and erected our tents, complete with lighting, platform, backdrops, coolants, etc. Some of my friends suggested we were crazy to plan an outdoor party at this time of year. I kept trusting God that no rain would fall on that day. I kept reminding God, Valsayn is known for having grand parties with no rain, so why when we decided to have a party, glorifying Him, should we have rain. Perhaps that got the enemy mad because the evening before the party we had a rain storm with thunder and lightning, completely blowing off the tents, scattering all our decorations, and making a swimming pool of the area. The area was a complete disaster and at one point we were thinking of moving to a church.

My daughter checked the weather forecast for the next day and it said heavy showers again with high winds. Instead of having a pity party we decided to have church. We sang, we clapped and rejoiced. We reminded God of all his rich promises to us. One of the songs we sang after listening to the weatherman was: "Whose Report Do You Believe?" We chose to believe the report of the Lord. We reminded God that this function was all about giving glory to Him so we could not fail. In our little room we held hands and committed the function into his hands. The night's weather forecast still did not deter us, because we knew it was all in God's hands.

The next day for the first time in 31 days, the sun came out and we gathered a team to clean up. There was no sign of what had taken place the day before. The guests arrived all decked off in their African outfits. Trini/African foods complete with wild game and Jolof rice were served, and we had an altogether great evening with the sounds of Christian music and drumming livening up Valsayn. Jesus Christ was glorified, and the devil was horrified. I kept saying to myself, "Lord, this one is for you."

Airport Favor: Gatwick

After traveling for hours in a sitting position, I would often suffer with swollen feet. On one occasion, I had come off a long flight from Europe and was about to take another ten-hour flight to Houston, Texas. In my usual manner, I spoke to the Lord telling him of my situation and asking him to do whatever in his power to get me a comfortable seat on the aircraft so that my already swollen legs would not explode.

After my nephew had checked me in at the airport, I was assigned to Gate 43A. I took my ticket and began my long walk in search of the gate. By this time, I'm no longer walking, but literally dragging with my heavy hand luggage. After a long walk that included going up and down escalators, I finally took the train and arrived at my gate. After about ten minutes of rest, I decided to check whether I was at the right gate. At that 99th hour, I realized that I was at the wrong gate through no fault of my own. The ticket said 43A but actually the flight was supposed to depart from another gate. The flight at the right gate which was miles away was about to take off. After bringing this error to the attention of an official, my entire status in the airport changed when they realized that the fault was their own.

I was immediately assigned a later flight, given VIP accommodation with accompanying food and drinks. I never knew that such luxurious accommodation existed in an airport. As somebody involved in the food industry, I took the opportunity to feast on all the various foods and drinks available at that lounge in Gatwick Airport. I spent the extra hours just walking around feasting my eyes and my stomach. To my surprise when the aircraft came, I was upgraded to business class with not only a comfortable seat, but a comfortable bed, as well, where I had the luxury of sleeping all the way to Houston.

The song on my heart was, "I keep falling in love with him, over and over, and over and over again. He grows sweeter and sweeter as the days go by; O what a love between my Lord and I; I keep falling in love with him, over and over, and over and over again."

"God never said that the journey would be easy,
but he did say that the arrival would be worthwhile."
Max Lucado.

CHAPTER 20
FINAL THOUGHTS

The road I have travelled has not always been an easy one, and the path was often full of stones, but I am still here. I know that the only reason I was able to make it this far, the only reason I am still here today, is the fact that God was walking the road with me every step of the way. When I called on him at a tender age in the midst of all my dilemma, he heard my cry and delivered me out of all my troubles. He is the same yesterday, today and forever more.

God isn't finished with me yet. I still have a lot to give and a lot to share. I firmly believe no matter where you come from and no matter the battles you face, with God's help, you can become someone who is an asset to his kingdom. Indeed, he will make you finish strong.

As the Apostle Paul so correctly stated: He who began a good work in you will complete it until the day of Jesus Christ (Philippians 1:6).

Prayer:

Gracious father, I want you to use all the experiences that have shaped my life - both good and bad for your glory. I am so grateful that you can use the mistakes and failures of my life. Help me to help others the way you have helped me.

Pearl Douglas-Spring

www.ingramcontent.com/pod-product-compliance
Lightning Source LLC
Chambersburg PA
CBHW040257170426
43192CB00020B/2835